POSITIVE
Leadership
PRINCIPLES
for Women

KAROL LADD

HARVEST HOUSE PUBLISHERS
EUGENE, OREGON

Cover by Koechel Peterson & Associates, Inc., Minneapolis, Minnesota

Back-cover author photo by Shooting Starr Photography by Cindi Starr. www.shootingstarrphotos.com

Karol Ladd is published in association with the literary agency of the Steve Laube Agency, LLC, 5025 N. Central Ave. #635, Phoenix, AZ 85012.

POSITIVE LEADERSHIP PRINCIPLES FOR WOMEN
Copyright © 2014 by Karol Ladd
Published by Harvest House Publishers
Eugene, Oregon 97402
www.harvesthousepublishers.com

ISBN 978-0-7369-5013-8 (hardcover)
ISBN 978-0-7369-5014-5 (eBook)

Printed in China

14 15 16 17 18 19 20 21 22 / RDS-JH / 10 9 8 7 6 5 4 3 2

Contents

Never Underestimate the Power of a Woman's Influence

*Who knows but that you have come to your
royal position for such a time as this?*

ESTHER 4:14

*If ever there comes a time when the women of the world
come together purely and simply for the benefit of mankind,
it will be a force such as the world has never known.*

MATTHEW ARNOLD

A recent survey of over 7000 leaders from high-performance companies revealed fascinating results concerning the effectiveness of women in leadership.[1] The survey showed that women outperformed men in 12 out of 16 leadership competencies! Women ranked higher than men in areas such as taking initiative, problem solving, building relationships, driving for results, and practicing self-development, to name a few.

Why do you think women seem to have these innate leadership qualities? What is it that stirs in the heart of a woman, motivating her to reach out to inspire others? I believe God has uniquely equipped us as women to feel things deeply and to care passionately about the world around us.

As women we have the opportunity to make a positive difference in our families, communities, and even our culture. All too often we are tempted to sit back and allow someone else to set the pace for the rest of society, but there has never been a more important time for us to lead with love and integrity. Whether you have the opportunity to be a leader within your neighborhood community, your family, your business, or your church, you have the potential to influence others through your words, ideas, and examples. My hope is that this book will light that fire of influence in your heart and encourage you to stand up and step out as an effective leader. Don't wait for someone else to carry out the job God has equipped you to do.

Perhaps you have never thought of yourself as the "leader type." Or maybe you are a reluctant leader who has been pushed into the position because no one else would take on the responsibility. Maybe you're a natural-born leader who seems to gravitate toward the top in every organization you join. In a way, as Christian women we all serve as leaders, because we are set apart, called to stand up for biblical principles and lead our culture by being an example of righteousness, love, and compassion.

Whether you are a reluctant leader, a natural-born one, or somewhere in between, you—and every one of us—can grow and develop fresh leadership skills in your life. In this book, I highlight eight principles that can be applied to your personal life as well as your professional one. Each of the principles opens up the door for us to positively influence the people around us. We will explore the lives of eight effective leaders in the Old Testament of the Bible. The time-tested principles we can glean from these powerful leaders have great implications for each of us no matter where we are in our faith journey.

I like to think of this volume as a pocket-sized book with a powerful punch. Each chapter is packed full of insightful stories and powerful principles to help you be an effective leader. At the end of each chapter you will find a recap of the positive principles, as well as several practical action points. You will also find a section with personal application questions to help you take what you have learned in the chapter and implement it in your current situation. You may want to give this book to others on your leadership team so you can study together and build a cohesive bond.

Do you think you could be—or do you know someone who might be—part of the next generation of leaders? I want to inspire and impact you to engage with the culture and relate to others in an effective way. Ultimately that's what leadership is all about—relationships. Certainly courage, character, vision, and wisdom all play a vital role in the makeup of a great leader, but if a leader does not have the power to relate well to others, their influence is diminished and their effectiveness weakened. The apostle Paul warned that if we set out to do great things without love, we are only resounding gongs or clanging cymbals. Now I don't know about you, but I don't have time to waste. I want my work to count, to be effective, to make a difference. *Love* is the difference.

My desire is that you will be encouraged to not only rise up and take on the position of service God has given you, but that you will also do it with extraordinary love. Our greatness in leadership comes as a result of our relationship with God—recognizing His great love for us and pouring that love out to others. *We* are not the greatest gift to this world, but *He* is! God did not intend for us to be celebrity leaders; He intends for us to be servant leaders. There is great joy and responsibility in serving as a leader.

The truth is, we don't serve alone. Just as God has called us to leadership, He will also walk with us through it. May you experience His love as you humbly lead others and make a difference in this world.

Do nothing out of selfish ambition or vain conceit.
Rather, in humility value others above yourselves,
not looking to your own interests
but each of you to the interests of the others.

Philippians 2:3-4

Chapter One

Rise to the Challenge

Making Your Mountains into Learning Experiences

*I press on toward the goal to win the prize for which
God has called me heavenward in Christ Jesus.*

Philippians 3:14

*I have learned that in every circumstance
that comes my way,
I can choose to respond in one of two ways:
I can whine or I can worship!*

Nancy Leigh DeMoss

When I was in high school, my mother took me to a lecture by Sir Edmund Hillary. I must admit, at the time I was not too excited about hearing some old guy talk about how he had climbed a mountain. It wasn't until he started speaking that I realized this man had accomplished a feat that was considered impossible. He had faced the seemingly insurmountable, pushed past the limitations, and climbed to the top of Mount Everest. Before his successful expedition in 1953, numerous groups had tried and failed to reach the summit. Even within his own expedition group, all but two of the climbers—he and Tenzing Norgay—turned back because of exhaustion at the high altitude.

Despite the obstacles, the discouragement, and even the abandonment by his group, Hillary persevered. His accomplishment was celebrated worldwide, and his influence inspired many others to reach toward their own personal goals. Oddly, Sir Edmund originally earned his living as a beekeeper in New Zealand. He started climbing mountains in his own country as a bit of a hobby. Little by little he progressed to climbing the Alps and eventually the Himalayas. The small mountains led to bigger mountains, preparing him to conquer the highest mountain—Mount Everest.

What are the mountains in your life? Mountains come in all shapes and sizes. They may be in the form of a difficult work relationship or a rebellious child or an overwhelming project that keeps you up at night. Some mountains may develop in our lives in the form of financial issues or a troubled marriage or even trying to lose weight. Actually, there are also mountains in our lives that aren't expressly negative; some of our greatest mountains may include such things as starting a new business or learning a new skill set or language.

As women, each mountain that we scale in life strengthens us and prepares us to face grander mountains ahead. Whether we choose the mountain or the mountain chooses us, we still have a choice as to how we will deal with it. We can either look at the mountains in our lives and grumble and complain about them, or we can choose to begin to climb them and conquer them. The secret to rising to the top of any mountain rests in our attitude and ability to persevere. Sir Edmund Hillary said, "It's not the mountain we conquer, but ourselves." From beekeeper to record breaker, Hillary conquered fears, discouragements, and failures. It didn't all happen at once, but he grew from each experience. We too can look at each mountain in our lives as an opportunity to grow and become stronger women.

No More Excuses

The story of Joseph in the Old Testament provides a poignant picture of a young man who found himself in the pit and yet reached the summit. Joseph went from the safe environment of home, to becoming a slave, and then to prison, and yet eventually to second in command of Egypt. It wasn't a smooth road, yet he scaled his personal mountains again and again. He didn't allow himself to get caught in the trap of blaming people or circumstances. He didn't spend time dwelling on the "if only" scenarios or mistakes in his life. Instead he moved forward and rose to the top of each circumstance in which God placed him.

Think about it—he could have easily rested on a big bed of excuses. His brothers had sold him into slavery, he had been unjustly punished, he was forgotten and abandoned. If anyone had a reason to give up and carry a chip on his shoulder, it was Joseph. Yet true leaders don't waste time making excuses for what they can't, won't, or couldn't do.

Stop for just a moment and consider the excuses rolling around in your head right now that keep you from climbing the mountain in front of you. Are you waiting for someone to change? Are you blaming someone else for your inability to move forward? Are you using your circumstances as an excuse? As we consider the story of Joseph, let's identify our own excuses and disarm them, not allowing them to get in the way of what God wants to do in our lives.

Perhaps you are familiar with Joseph's story. He was one of twelve brothers, and he was dearly loved by his father, Jacob. In fact, as the favorite son (never a good idea to institute in a family) he was given a coat of honor by his dad—a coat of many colors. Of course this only instilled more jealousy and anger in the hearts of his brothers. When the opportunity was right, the brothers threw Joseph into a pit and sold him to slave traders from Egypt. Here was a boy who had once lived in the comfort of his own home, most honored by his father, and now he was abandoned and forced into slavery at the cruel hand of his brothers.

I don't know about you, but I would have started feeling sorry for myself right there. I would have been tempted to give up hope, yet Joseph handled this mountain a little differently. He didn't succumb to the temptation to feel sorry for himself and wallow in discouragement. Instead he jumped into his situation with both feet, embraced the challenge, and rose to the top. It's as if he said, "This is where I'm at right now, so I'll make the best of it." He was sold to an Egyptian named Potiphar, and here he climbed to the top of his first mountain. The Bible describes his climb this way:

> The LORD was with Joseph so that he prospered, and he lived in the house of his Egyptian master. When his master saw that the LORD was with him and that the LORD gave him success in everything he did, Joseph found favor in his eyes and became his attendant. Potiphar put him in charge of his household, and he entrusted to his care everything he owned. From the time he put him in charge of his household and of all that he owned, the LORD blessed the household of the

Egyptian because of Joseph. The blessing of the LORD was on everything Potiphar had, both in the house and in the field. So Potiphar left everything he had in Joseph's care; with Joseph in charge, he did not concern himself with anything except the food he ate. [1]

God shined His favor on Joseph and blessed his work, but keep in mind that Joseph had to do the work. He didn't lazily sit around hoping God would do it all for him. He was responsible and trustworthy to the point that Potiphar put him in charge of everything. He didn't have family or friends there to offer encouragement and support. He didn't have inside connections or favors from those in authority to make his promotion happen. He had God, and God was his help and his companion. Joseph did his work with excellence and proved himself to be a faithful servant, and God blessed his work.

During his time in Potiphar's household, Joseph learned administrative responsibilities, accounting, logistics, and managerial skills, among other valuable lessons. He was in charge of both Potiphar's house and his field, which was an important training ground to prepare him to lead Egypt one day. It was a small mountain preparation for the big mountain of being in charge of all the storehouses of Egypt, yet it was a mountain within the confines of slavery. He didn't choose this mountain, but with God's help he was able to climb it and make the most of a difficult situation.

Perhaps you feel stuck in a situation that seems hopeless or circumstances that don't seem to be utilizing all your gifts and talents. Pay attention to the training God is giving you right where you are. Don't try to rush Him and move ahead of what He is teaching you. God doesn't waste any experience in our lives. What may seem like a mistake could be just the situation He wants to use to prepare you for your next role in leadership. Let's get in the habit of asking the question, "God, what do You want to teach me here?"

Joseph not only learned administrative skills, but he also learned humility and dependence on God. He grew in integrity as well. Imagine trusting someone so much that you completely put him or her in charge of everything! Do you have someone like that in your life? Let's admit it—that kind of person is rare. Joseph proved himself faithful in the small tasks in order to be put in charge of the greater ones. Yes, he had climbed the bitter mountain of slavery, overcoming the loss of his comfortable life and family, and he found himself at the pinnacle—the top of the household.

Sadly, there are times when we get thrown off the mountaintop, sometimes not by our own doing. Falling off the mountain doesn't mean it's over. God is there to break the fall, care for us, and put us on the path again. Joseph lived a life of integrity and honor, but we can't say the same about Potiphar's wife. She was attracted to Joseph and tried to entice him to sleep with her. He refused, saying, "With me in charge...my master does not concern himself with anything in the house; everything he owns he has entrusted to my care. No one is greater in this house than I am. My master has withheld nothing from me except you, because you are his wife. How then could I do such a wicked thing and sin against God?"[2]

Notice that Joseph recognized this kind of action was a sin against God. He had a healthy fear of the Lord, which is the very foundation of wisdom. Joseph not only knew who God was, but he also wanted to walk in obedience to Him. A godly leader has a sense of God's presence and a recognition that they ultimately answer to

Him. Joseph knew he answered to a higher calling. A woman with a deep sense of integrity does what is right even when no one is around to see, because she knows she answers to God, not people.

Potiphar's wife became angry at Joseph and accused him of rape. He was thrown in prison for a crime he didn't commit. Welcome to your next mountain, Joseph! He found himself at the base of the mountain of unjust accusations, misunderstanding, dishonor, discouragement, and imprisonment. At this point it would have been easy to throw in the towel, stay in the valley, and be filled with anger, hatred, and revenge for everyone throughout his life who had done him wrong. If this were a Hollywood movie, the Joseph character would have probably reacted with revenge, but not the real man. Instead we see him put on his hiking boots and begin to scale the next mountain.

Lessons Learned Outside Our Comfort Zone

Recently I had the opportunity to visit the Gospel for Asia headquarters and seminary in India. The young women at the seminary live a beautifully disciplined and devoted life to the Lord. On their faces I saw a true joy in the Lord as they surrendered their lives to His service. One thing I will always remember were the thatched huts on campus that served as classrooms for the students. The reason the classes met in thatched huts was to help the students experience the feel of what it would be like for them as they went into tribal areas and out of the comfort of seminary. It was a visual reminder of the surroundings they would face in the future.[3]

Comparing those thatched huts to the nice comfortable classrooms we have in college here in the states, I think I would choose nice and comfy. Isn't that what we want life to be like? "Lord, help me to grow and be a great leader, but could You do it in a nice, cozy, happy environment without any discomfort or challenges?" You know, as well as I do, that some of the most important lessons happen in the "thatched huts" of life. Once again, God prepared Joseph for a higher mountain by taking him to the classroom of discomfort.

It's hard to imagine what prisons were like in 1800 BC Egypt. I'm going to assume that Joseph's prison wasn't the nicest of environments, certainly lacking the comforts of Potiphar's home or the life Joseph once knew with his father. Yet in this dungeon classroom, God was with Joseph, teaching and training him for greater leadership and important service on a higher level. Once again, he was faithful in his responsibilities and worked with excellence even in the small prison tasks he was given. He was faithful in the small things! God showed him kindness and gave him success once again.

Here's what we read in Genesis:

> While Joseph was there in the prison, the LORD was with him; he showed him kindness and granted him favor in the eyes of the prison warden. So the warden put Joseph in charge of all those held in the prison, and he was made responsible for all that was done there. The warden paid no attention to anything under Joseph's care, because the LORD was with Joseph and gave him success in whatever he did.[4]

What lessons did Joseph acquire here that he had not already learned in Potiphar's house? Here, in prison, his faith was bolstered as he experienced the continued faithfulness of the Lord. God was with him and blessed him in the midst of this dark time. He became confident that even in the dark valleys, God was always there and would not leave him. Joseph most likely learned humility and compassion as he reached out and touched the other prisoners and cared for their needs. He developed a servant's heart. He became resourceful with the little that he had. Most important, he learned patience, and the value of waiting on the Lord's timing.

While he was in prison, two of his fellow prisoners had perplexing dreams. Joseph told them, "Do not interpretations belong to God? Tell me your dreams."[5] Notice his simple reliance on God. Joseph's focus was on God, and he was confident in what God could do. Once Joseph interpreted the dreams, one of the prisoners was released and sent back to his post with the Pharaoh of Egypt. Joseph asked the prisoner to remember him once he was back in the position of serving in the royal court, but the freed prisoner forgot. What an opportunity for Joseph to depend on God and not man, and wait on God's perfect timing.

God's Plan Is Best

Eventually, Pharaoh had a dream and Joseph's prison friend remembered him. Joseph was called before Pharaoh to interpret the dream. As a result of properly interpreting Pharaoh's dream about the seven years of growth and subsequent seven years of famine, Joseph was elevated to second in command. He was put in an administrative position to direct the storage of goods in order to prepare for the years of famine. God took Joseph to the top of the mountain! It was time. He was ready. God had taught him and prepared him through the classrooms of suffering so that he would have the skills to lead and oversee the entire land of Egypt. He was wise, organized, and resourceful as a result of his earlier mountain climbs. As a leader of Egypt he was responsible, efficient, and he ruled with integrity.

Most important, Joseph did not hold a grudge. He moved on, forgetting the past and releasing the entanglement of hatred and bitterness. One of my favorite passages in all of Scripture is found at the end of his story and reveals the secret to his ability to rise above his circumstances. In the end, he was reunited with his brothers and father. After his father passed away, his brothers feared that Joseph would retaliate and take revenge on them for their past cruelty toward him. He responded in grace, "'Don't be afraid. Am I in the place of God? You intended to harm me, but God intended it for good to accomplish what is now being done, the saving of many lives. So then, don't be afraid. I will provide for you and your children.' And he reassured them and spoke kindly to them."[6]

No anger, no revenge, only kindness. Why? Because Joseph knew that God had a plan all along. His eyes were on God and His plan, not on the pettiness of his brothers. When Joseph was just a boy, he had a dream that his brothers would one day bow down to him. God had set this vision in his heart, and Joseph never forgot it.

What vision has God given you? Don't lose sight of it, but more important, don't lose sight of your dependence on Him. He has a plan. Even through the dark times when you feel as though your mountain is too difficult, you can trust Him. He has not left you.

Let us see the mountains in front of us as opportunities to learn and grow. They are in our lives not to discourage us, but rather to strengthen us and prepare us for bigger mountains in the future. The powerful theologian C.H. Spurgeon faced many personal mountains in his own life. He wrote, "If you would find the men who serve God the best, you must look for the men of the most faith. Little faith will save a man, but little faith cannot do great things for God."[7] How does our little faith grow into big faith? It happens as we climb the mountains in front of us, depending on God every step of the way.

Think Pink

Mary Crowley, founder of Home Interiors & Gifts (now part of the company Celebrating Home), was one of the premier Christian businesswomen of Dallas, Texas. Her life was not an easy journey, but as a woman with a firm faith in God, she grew and learned through each struggle in her life. Married in 1932 and with children coming soon after that, she and her husband struggled to survive through the Depression. Mary realized that if she was going to be able to feed her family, she would need to find work. Although jobs were scarce at the time, especially for women, Mary chose a store she wanted to work in, dressed up and armed herself with a confident smile, walked in the doors of the store, and got the job!

Although she didn't realize it at the time, this job enabled Mary to develop a shrewd business sense that later prepared her to become head of a multimillion-dollar company. Sadly, her marriage crumbled in 1939. She began studying to be a CPA and worked full-time at an insurance company. Additionally, Mary suffered from insomnia, yet she turned her problems over to God. She used to pray, "Lord, You know I've got to get my rest. You worry about these problems. You're going to be up all night anyway." She would then go to sleep, leaving her problems in God's hands. Her faith in Him never wavered, and she found her confidence and strength in Him during those lean years.

In 1948 she married David Crowley Jr., whom she had met at the insurance company. As a newlywed, Mary wanted to make her home as attractive as she could despite her limited funds. She took a job as an accountant in a furniture company, and soon she began to notice that when people came to buy furniture, they had no idea how to accessorize their new furniture. Ideas began to dance around in her mind as to how she could help these people, but she also longed to be home with her children. In God's way and in His timing, He began to put it all together. Several years later, a man who imported gifts and decorative accessories asked Mary to become his sales manager in a new direct-sales company.

After working with this company for only three years, Mary's staff had increased to 500 women selling accessories through home parties. Sounds like a Joseph-type success, doesn't it? The owner was pleased, but he decided to add cocktail parties to the company functions, and he put limits on the commissions the saleswomen could make. Mary told him she didn't agree with these conditions, so he sent her the office furniture that belonged to her and told her he was done with her position. Mary grieved the loss of being tossed off of that mountain, but she trusted God and knew He had a plan.

It was then that she founded her own company, Home Interiors & Gifts. She followed God's leading, and she gave Him credit for the success of her company. She knew that it was He who opened the doors, but it was her responsibility to walk through them. Mary's desire was to help woman and minister to their needs. Many of the women who became a part of her team had never held jobs before and even needed help with their appearance. Soon the company was helping women both personally and financially, paying dividends and bonuses. The business continued to grow, and in 1962, the sales force recorded one million dollars in sales. Sadly, in that same year Mary was diagnosed with cancer. She ended up fighting two bouts (mountains if you will) of cancer, but continued to go forward and bless many women in the process.

Mary was one of the first women to serve on the board of directors of the Billy Graham Evangelistic Association. She received two honorary doctorate degrees before her death in 1986.[8] Today, the Mary Crowley Cancer Research Centers in Dallas provide hope to cancer patients by expanding treatment options through investigational vaccine, gene, and cellular therapies. Just as God used the mountains in Joseph's life to eventually save many generations to come, so the Lord used the life of Mary Crowley to impact the lives of women and bring hope to generations of cancer patients as well.

=== *Positive Leadership Strategy* ===

POWERFUL TRUTH

God uses the obstacles in our lives to prepare us for leadership, building courage, character, and confidence.

PRACTICAL APPLICATION

Embrace the mountains in front of you and see them as opportunities for growth.

Don't blame others or make excuses.

Do your work with excellence and integrity.

Be faithful in the small tasks.

Always ask, "Lord what do You want me to learn here?"

Keep your eyes on God's plan for you.

Personalize It

1. What mountain are you currently facing in your leadership role?

2. What is God teaching you personally through this challenge?

3. How can you thank God specifically for this mountain?

Chapter Two

Change Your Focus

Managing Around Your Weaknesses

*His divine power has given us everything
we need for a godly life
through our knowledge of him who called us
by his own glory and goodness.*

2 Peter 1:3-4

*For every failure, there's an alternative course of action.
You just have to find it. When you come
to a roadblock, take a detour.*

Mary Kay Ash

As a young woman with Down syndrome, Lisa focuses on her abilities and not her limitations. Lisa wanted to be a singer from the time she was a little girl, but her mother realized that her daughter was not "blessed with a voice for publicly singing," as she lovingly puts it. Instead of telling Lisa what she shouldn't do, her mom began to explore what Lisa could do. She talked to a sign language teacher named Marla and asked her to teach Lisa one song. Lisa picked a song sung by Sandi Patty entitled "In Heaven's Eyes." After only one lesson, she had learned to sign the whole song! Marla quickly recognized that Lisa had a gift. Now Lisa knows over 300 songs in sign language.

Lisa is one young lady with big faith in an Almighty God. She knows that He has given her a gift, and so she doesn't limit the possibilities of what He can do through a girl with Down syndrome. She has shared her story with audiences of thousands and loves to inspire others to discover their God-given potential. She has had the honor of accompanying Christian song artists like Sandi Patty, Kathy Troccoli, and Avalon—just to name a few. She has also traveled around the country with Women of Faith, using sign language to accompany their worship teams.

How did Lisa get her start? It started with her love for Sandi Patty's music. Lisa went to Sandi's concerts as a child and sat in the front row, signing to her songs. One year she was able to meet the singer in person and told her she would love to sign for her. The very next year Sandi came back to the area for a Christmas concert, and there was Lisa on the front row again! Out of the blue, Sandi motioned for Lisa to join her on stage. She asked her if she knew two of her songs, and Lisa said she knew *all* of Sandi's songs. Sandi said, "Come on, let's go…take a deep breath." Lisa courageously stepped into the limelight and signed the words to the songs. All the people in the audience cheered and showed their pleasure by a standing ovation. The rest is history.

❧

Like Lisa, we are all equipped with God-given gifts, talents, and abilities. They may not be as publically appreciated as Lisa's gifts, but they are significant just the same. The challenge for most of us is this: often we are so focused on what we can't do that we miss what we are able to do. Sure, everyone has weaknesses and inabilities, yet if we can learn how to manage around our limitations, then we can use our strengths for the glory of God. It's sad to think how many women concentrate on their limitations instead of realizing their full potential.

With a thankful heart, I can reflect on the people in my own life who spoke words of encouragement to me and helped me see some of my abilities. I hope you have those kinds of people in your life too. There will always be thoughts inside our head from the enemy trying to keep us boxed in by our inabilities. Don't listen to that voice! Instead, build on the truth that God created you, fashioned you, and designed you for a purpose. He will equip you for what He has created you to do. Take a moment right now to thank the Lord for the unique gifts He has given you.

What Does God Want You to Do?

Perhaps you have heard the phrase "Where God guides, He provides." I've also heard it said, "If God has called you to it, He will see you through it." Perhaps these short maxims would have been helpful to Moses when he was called to leadership at the burning bush. His story begins as he was tending his father-in-law's sheep. Moses saw a strange sight, a bush that was on fire but wasn't burning. As he approached the bush, God called to him. Here we begin to see a glimpse of God's great power and holiness. The Lord told Moses to stay back and take off his sandals, because the place on which he was standing was holy ground. He proceeded to introduce Himself to Moses: "I am the God of your father, the God of Abraham, the God of Isaac and the God of Jacob."[1] Moses hid his face, because he was afraid to look at God.

This was a life-defining moment for Moses. He had heard about God, but now he was having a conversation with the Almighty One Himself. Oh, what a dramatic picture! Imagine yourself in his place, overcome with awe and humility. In this incredibly glorious encounter, God was calling Moses for a specific purpose—a monumental purpose. He was to lead the Israelite nation out of bondage and into the Promised Land. Understandably, Moses asked, "Who am I that I should go to Pharaoh and bring the Israelites out of Egypt?"[2] Personally, we may find ourselves asking the very same question when we realize God's call: "Who am I, that I should take on this leadership position?"

Kindly, God reassured Moses, "I will be with you."

He told Moses His credentials, "I AM WHO I AM. This is what you are to say to the Israelites: 'I AM has sent me to you.'"[3] In other words, *I am the God who always was, who always will be, and who is here with you now. I am the all-sufficient One; you need no other.* God told Moses to step out in faith and go to Pharaoh. He even told him what to say, and what He was planning to do.

Now at this point you would think Moses would feel a sense of confidence based on who God is and what He had said. But fear seemed to be winning the battle against faith in his mind. Been there?

After God's reassuring words Moses replied with this question: "What if they do not believe me or listen to me and say, 'The LORD did not appear to you'?"[4] I know I've played out a few what-if scenarios in my mind as well. Worries and assumptions can work their way into our thought life and diminish our focus and faith on the Lord. Aren't you glad He is patient with us? He loves us and gently brings us to a place of faith. God decided to perform a few miracles right then and there so Moses' faith would be bolstered as he observed God's power. God changed Moses' staff into a snake and then back into a rod again. Next, He told Moses to put his hand inside his cloak, and when he pulled it out it was leprous. Then God restored his hand.

At this point, you would think that Moses would be ready to say, "Let's go for it! I've got the power of God on my side! He is with me and will lead through me! Thank You, God, for equipping me for this job You called me to do." Well, that's not exactly the response he had. Instead of focusing on the power of God, Moses began to think about his inabilities and weaknesses. He said to the Lord, "Pardon your servant, Lord. I have never been eloquent, neither in the past nor since you have spoken to your servant. I am slow of speech and tongue."[5]

So God responded, "Who gave human beings their mouths? Who makes them deaf or mute? Who gives them sight or makes them blind? Is it not I, the LORD? Now go; I will help you speak and will teach you what to say."[6] Can you imagine the Creator of all the universe reminding you that He is the One who equips you and gives you what you need for your role as a leader? What a powerfully motivating statement. God is aware of our weaknesses. He made us. He designed us. Notice that He said He makes some deaf and mute. Some with sight and some without. Have you ever thought about the fact that God gave you certain abilities and also certain inabilities? Why would He do that?

We cannot understand all of God's purposes and why He allows us to have personal weaknesses or inabilities in our lives. For Moses, it was slowness of speech. For another person it may be a physical challenge or an emotional setback. Yet one truth we can recognize is that God uses us despite our weaknesses or inabilities. Each personal challenge and each handicap we face as leaders can point us back to our dependence on God and our need for Him. Our weaknesses often keep us from becoming proud or thinking we can do things on our own strength.

I'm reminded of the apostle Paul, who said,

> In order to keep me from becoming conceited, I was given a thorn in my flesh, a messenger of Satan, to torment me. Three times I pleaded with the Lord to take it away from me. But he said to me, "My grace is sufficient for you, for my power is made perfect in weakness." Therefore I will boast all the more gladly about my weaknesses, so that Christ's power may rest on me. That is why, for Christ's sake, I delight in weaknesses, in insults, in hardships, in persecutions, in difficulties. For when I am weak, then I am strong.[7]

Thank the Lord for Your Strengths and Weaknesses

Did you notice that Paul said he would gladly boast about his weaknesses so the power of God could rest on him? It's easy to thank God for the gifts He has given us, but we can also thank Him for our weaknesses because they keep us looking to Him and leaning in on Him. Sadly, Moses wasn't thanking God for his weaknesses. Nope. Instead he just kept letting his fears distract him from moving forward in the role of leadership God had given him. Even after God specifically said, "I will help you speak and will teach you what to say," Moses replied, "Pardon your servant, Lord. Please send someone else."[8]

Uh-oh! Perhaps Moses tested God's patience a little too much. Here's how the conversation finally came to a close:

> Then the LORD's anger burned against Moses and he said, "What about your brother, Aaron the Levite? I know he can speak well. He is already on his way to meet you, and he will be glad to see you. You shall speak to him and put words in his mouth; I will help both of you speak and will teach you what to do. He will speak to the people for you, and it will be as if he were your mouth and as if you were God to him. But take this staff in your hand so you can perform the signs with it."[9]

God decided to send Moses' brother Aaron to help him. The amazing thing to me is that the Lord still used Moses despite his lack of faith. He didn't use him in just a little way; He used him in a big, mighty way!

Thank You, Lord, that despite our fears or our lack of faith and trust, You still equip us and use us for kingdom purposes. You even work beyond our weakness of fear and self-doubt. Oh Lord, help us to be willing vessels when You call us. Help us to see Your power at work in our lives and not be overwhelmed by our weaknesses.

God was well aware of Moses' weakness in the form of self-doubt. The Scripture tells us that Aaron was on his way to meet Moses even as they were having their conversation. Did you catch that? God had already made provision for Moses before he asked. God lovingly provided Aaron to help Moses speak, but He still gave Moses the leadership role and authority.

What is God calling you to do? Have you been avoiding the call because you are concerned about your shortcomings and inabilities? All of us have limitations. Let's turn our eyes away from what we see as our flaws, and turn instead to our loving and powerful God, who created us. He knows exactly what we need. He will equip us for the role He has given us. Keep your eyes on Him and His character and His abilities. Seek His power and strength to accomplish what He has put in front of you. Most important, thank Him for your weaknesses, because they keep you humble and keep you turning toward Him.

Many years later, after Moses had led the Israelites out of Egypt and into the wilderness, we find a little-known story of an encounter with his brother, Aaron, and sister, Miriam. The two criticized Moses and questioned his leadership. Through the conflict we see a glowing statement of Moses' character. Recorded in Numbers 12 we find this nugget of truth: "Moses was a very humble man, more humble than anyone else on the face of the earth."[10] Now let me remind you that it was Moses who wrote that statement! It doesn't seem so humble to say that about yourself, right? That is, until you begin to examine the word Moses used. It is the Hebrew word *anayv*, which is often translated "meek." It implies that "he was entirely dependent on God."

With this in mind, consider what Moses was really saying of himself: "Moses was entirely dependent on God, more dependent on God than anyone else on the face of the earth." What a powerful statement! This is the secret behind his ability to lead the Israelites. It wasn't his own strength, but God's strength on which he leaned. He was well aware of his weaknesses, but he had grown to a point of entirely depending on God.

What will you do with your weaknesses? Will you use them as an excuse, or will you give them over to God and ask Him to show Himself strong despite your weaknesses? It may be that He will bring someone to help you, or it may mean that He does the mighty work in you. Either way, the message is clear—great leaders don't focus on their shortcomings, but rather they depend entirely on God for His strength.

Positive Leadership Strategy

POWERFUL TRUTH

Get your eyes off of what you can't do, and turn your focus toward what God can do.

PRACTICAL APPLICATION

Thank God for the gifts He has given you.

Listen to His direction.

Remember, where God guides, He provides.

Lean on Him, knowing He is with you.

Give your weaknesses over to God and stop worrying about them.

Thank Him for your weaknesses, as they lead you to depend on Him for strength.

Personalize It

1. What are the gifts God has given you? Take a moment to thank the Lord in all humility for those gifts.

2. How is He directing you to use your gifts?

3. Who are the people in your life right now who need to be encouraged in their gifts?

Chapter Three

Step Forward with Courage

Walking into New Territory with God-Confidence

Cheer up…! Don't be afraid!
For the Lord *your God*
is living among you.
He is a mighty savior.

Zephaniah 3:16 nlt

You gain strength, courage, and
confidence by every experience
in which you really stop to look fear in the face.
You must do the thing you think you cannot do.

Eleanor Roosevelt

Born into slavery in Dorchester County, Maryland, Harriet experienced a painful and difficult life as a young girl. She was often whipped and beaten, and at one point she was hit in the head by a heavy metal weight, causing a severe head injury with lifelong complications. She had powerful dream experiences as a result of her head injuries, and as a devout Christian she ascribed the vivid dreams as revelations from God.

When she was almost 30 years old, Harriet escaped to Philadelphia, but she soon returned to her home in Maryland to rescue her family. Slowly and courageously, she started leading one group at a time out of the state, and eventually she guided dozens of slaves to their freedom through the network known as the Underground Railroad. Harriet claimed that she "never lost a passenger" as she traveled by night helping slaves to their freedom. Many affectionately called her "Moses" for leading so many out of slavery and into freedom and hope.

Harriet Tubman was not one to sit still or let fear overtake her. When the American Civil War began, she worked for the Union army serving as a cook and a nurse, but later as an armed scout and a spy. She was the first woman to lead an armed expedition in the war. She guided the Combahee River Raid, liberating more than 700 slaves in South Carolina. Harriet was one brave woman!

After the war, she retired to her family's home in Auburn, New York, and cared for her aging parents. But she never really stopped fighting. She became active in the women's suffrage movement in New York. As she neared the end of her life, she moved into a home for elderly African-Americans that she had helped start years earlier. When she died, she was buried with military honors at Fort Hill Cemetery in Auburn. Despite her difficulties, Harriet Tubman was a courageous leader who was always thinking of the needs of others.

Author M. Scott Peck described courage in this way, "Courage is not the absence of fear; it is the making of action in spite of fear, the moving against the resistance engendered by fear into the unknown and into the future."[1] Certainly, Harriet Tubman is an example of a woman who loved people and didn't allow fear to get in the way of what she knew God had called her to do. So how do we learn to master our fears? How can we be strong and courageous in our leadership roles? Let's look at a unique portrait of a fearless leader in the Old Testament who found his strength from God.

Led by God

It must have seemed crazy. Joshua was instructed to lead a multitude of "wilderness wanderers" across an overflowing river in order to defeat a giant walled city by simply walking around it and blowing trumpets. Really? Who came up with that idea? Well, the short answer is—Almighty God. And when it's God's plan we can trust in all certainty that it will work. Let's take a look at God's preparation of Joshua. The narrative is found in the book of Joshua in the Old Testament. Here we read the plan for victory given directly from God to Joshua:

> After the death of Moses the servant of the LORD, the LORD said to Joshua son of Nun, Moses' aide: "Moses my servant is dead. Now then, you and all these people, get ready to cross the Jordan River into the land I am about to give to them—to the Israelites. I will give you every place where you set your foot, as I promised Moses. Your territory will extend from the desert to Lebanon, and from the great river, the Euphrates— all the Hittite country—to the Mediterranean Sea in the west. No one will be able to stand against you all the days of your life. As I was with Moses, so I will be with you; I will never leave you nor forsake you. Be strong and courageous, because you will lead these

people to inherit the land I swore to their ancestors to give them."[2]

What a powerfully positive charge given to Joshua! Not only did God tell him that He would give the Israelites victory, but He also offered that great statement of comfort He had also spoken to Moses: "I will be with you." It has been said that those five words are possibly the greatest motivational statement ever uttered. There is great comfort from fear, great help in affliction, when we know that we are not alone. God doesn't say that everything we do will be wonderful, smooth, or successful, but He does promise that He will be with us through the dark moments. As David wrote in Psalm 23, "Even though I walk through the darkest valley, I will fear no evil, for you are with me; your rod and your staff, they comfort me."[3]

Continually throughout Scripture, we see the charge "Do not be afraid" coupled with the assurance "I am with you." As followers of Christ, this is true faith—to trust that no matter what lies down the road ahead, God will be with us. His presence, guidance, and direction offer the comfort and care we need. Fear disappears when our faith in Him prevails in our hearts and minds. Edmund Burke said, "No passion so effectually robs the mind of all its powers of acting and reasoning as fear."[4] Fear has the potential to render us useless. It can keep us from moving forward with God's plan, and that's why it is so destructive. It is the opposite of trusting God's presence and His care for us.

The battle against fear begins in the mind. What fears do you have attacking your thought-life right now? When you consider God's presence, how does that change the strongholds of fear? As we consider His presence, one thing becomes clear—if we are living in disobedience or sin, it is difficult to take joy in His presence. What I am saying is that if we are rebelling against Him and living in disobedience to His Word, we may not find comfort by focusing on His presence—in fact we may want to run the other way. There is a strong connection between walking in obedience to Him and stepping forward courageously in His power. God not only charged Joshua to step forward in faith, but He also instructed him to stay close in obedience. The two go hand in hand.

Walking with Him

Notice the instructions God gave Joshua:

> Be strong and very courageous. Be careful to obey all the law my servant Moses gave you; do not turn from it to the right or to the left, that you may be successful wherever you go. Keep this Book of the Law always on your lips; meditate on it day and night, so that you may be careful to do everything written in it. Then you will be prosperous and successful. Have I not commanded you? Be strong and courageous. Do not be afraid; do not be discouraged, for the Lord your God will be with you wherever you go.[5]

God commanded Joshua to be a man of the Scriptures. He wanted Joshua to live in obedience to Him so he could lead others to do the same. But Joshua needed to know God's Word in order to obey it. He was instructed to have it always on his lips, meditating on it day and night, so that he would continually be living it out. God charged Joshua to stay in His Word, and not turn to the right or to the left. In other words, Joshua was to be careful to never veer from God's instructions, even slightly.

And twice in this passage we see God's promise that Joshua would be successful and prosperous. There are two Hebrew words used in the text to translate "successful and prosperous." The first is *sakal*, which means "to be prudent, act wisely, give attention to, ponder, prosper." The second is *tsaleach*, which generally expresses the idea of a successful venture as contrasted with failure. The source of such success is God.

It is important to understand what God is saying here. This is not a blanket statement to all of us that if we obey Him, everything in our lives will be grand and prosperous. We know that trials come to even the most obedient of His servants. God was giving a specific promise to Joshua that the result of his obedience to God's laws would mean that he would be prudent and act wisely, and he would have a successful venture.

As a general statement to us all, the result of obeying God's Word is that we act wisely and prudently and as a result experience success. And God's definition of success may be slightly different than our own. Success in His eyes is obedience to Him—so our success may mean lovingly bringing our neighbors dinner, or faithfully staying in a challenging marriage, or diligently preparing to teach fifth-grade Sunday school. The world has a different view of success—big house, nice car, large bank account, fame and recognition. Think about it— how do you personally define success?

The question we should be asking is not, "What kind of success is God going to grant me?" I believe the more important question is,

"Am I successful in His eyes?" For Joshua, success began in knowing and meditating on God's Word so that it permeated his very being. So we must ask ourselves, do we know and meditate on His Word? Is it such a part of our lives that it is on our lips continually? And are we living it out in our daily lives?

To meditate on God's Word means reading it with thoughtfulness, lingering over it, dwelling on it, and pondering it. Take even a small passage of Scripture daily and allow it to permeate your thoughts and actions. One of the best ways I've found to meditate on God's Word day and night is through memorizing it. I know, I know that's the last thing you wanted to read, but it's had a powerful impact on my life. God's Word has become very personal and alive to me through memorizing passages, and I'm able to readily share them with others.

There are times at night when I may have trouble falling asleep, tossing and turning with the cares of the day. It is at that point I start reciting scriptures in my mind, and a beautiful peace comes over me. How wonderful to fall asleep with God's Word on my heart and mind. If you are wondering where to start, why not memorize the verses that are found at the beginning of each of the chapters of this book? As leaders, we can strengthen others through the power of God's Word, and when we have it memorized it flows out of us.*

God told Joshua to meditate on His Word, but He also told him to obey it! In the book of Numbers we read a description of Joshua written by Moses: "Joshua…followed the Lord wholeheartedly."[6]

---

* For tips on how to memorize Scripture, visit my website, www.KarolLadd.com, for a free download on the topic.

That means he followed God with his whole being. He was sold out and ready for action. You may remember that he was one of two spies who looked at the Promised Land with faith in God, while all the rest of the spies feared the giants in the land. God placed him in charge of leading the Israelites because he was focused on God's character, not the enemies' height. Can the description of Joshua describe us as well? Can it be said that we follow the Lord wholeheartedly? Or are we the kind of women who just "play church" on Sunday mornings because it looks good? Or are we all in—with our heart, mind, soul, and strength?

Not Alone

As far as battle strategies go, it doesn't seem like a good plan to conquer a city by simply walking around it seven times. Most armies would put up siege ramps and ladders to scale the walls and overwhelm the enemy. Yet we know that when God is fighting our battles, the weapons of warfare are a little different. The key is that Joshua was listening to God's guidance and instruction, not his own silly whims or random ideas. He had to trust a plan that did not make human sense. But it did make God-sense. What was required of Joshua? Faith, obedience, and listening to God. Instead of employing the latest battle techniques, Joshua had to walk with God. We too must guard against doing things just because that's the way everyone else would do it. We can certainly seek wise counsel from others and learn the best job practices, but in the end our responsibility as godly leaders is to listen to His voice.

The Bible tells us that Joshua had an encounter with God the night before the battle of Jericho. Here's the account found in Joshua 5 and 6:

> When Joshua was near Jericho, he looked up and saw a man standing in front of him with a drawn sword in his hand. Joshua went up to him and asked, "Are you for us or for our enemies?"
>
> "Neither," he replied, "but as commander of the army of the LORD I have now come." Then Joshua fell facedown to the ground in reverence, and asked him, "What message does my Lord have for his servant?"
>
> The commander of the LORD's army replied, "Take off your sandals, for the place where you are standing is holy." And Joshua did so...
>
> Then the LORD said to Joshua, "See, I have delivered Jericho into your hands, along with its king and its fighting men. March around the city once with all the armed men. Do this for six days. Have seven priests carry trumpets of rams' horns in front of the ark. On the seventh day, march around the city seven times, with the priests blowing the trumpets. When you hear them sound a long blast on the trumpets, have the whole army give a loud shout; then the wall of the city will collapse and the army will go up, everyone straight in."[7]

Talk about a power meeting! Joshua was talking to a Man who called Himself the Commander of the Lord's Army. Well, the Commander of the Lord's Army is God! This was none other than God in the flesh, Jesus. Yes, Jesus had come to reassure Joshua and give him final instructions before the battle. He used the words, "I have delivered Jericho into your hands." It was as good as done! If God said it, it was true even before it happened. He made it clear that it was His battle and that He was their deliverer.

Interestingly, there is one other place where God told someone to take off their sandals. When Moses encountered God at the burning bush, God gave the same instructions. Now keep in mind that Joshua was Moses' right-hand man throughout the 40 years in the wilderness. I'm sure Moses told him about the burning bush experience a time or two. As God gave those same instructions to Joshua, I believe He was reassuring him that the same holy and powerful God who had been with Moses was also going deliver him in battle.

The Bible tells us that Joshua and the Israelites did exactly what God instructed them to do. When they shouted, the walls collapsed. The Israelites were powerless, but God was powerful. It was His work in His way. Isn't that a picture of salvation? We didn't do the work; Christ did the work on the cross. What a beautiful reminder that the battle over sin and death was won by Jesus because we are powerless to win that battle on our own. But this story also is a reminder that we do not face our battles alone. Jesus goes before us. Our job is to listen and obey. A leader who steps out in faith must also walk in step with God's Word. Joshua was a courageous leader because he was a man of faith who listened to God. Are you listening?

Powerful Truth

Stepping out in faith requires walking in step with God.

Practical Application

Identify your fears, but don't dwell on them.
Build your faith through meditating on God's Word.
Follow God's commands and directions for your life.
Courageously take steps forward.
Memorize God's Word for constant encouragement.
Fill your mind with God's promises.

Personalize It

1. What fears do you have lurking in your mind right now? Take time to pray and give each of these areas over to the Lord, thanking Him for His presence in your life.

2. What truth about God can you focus on instead of the fear?

3. How do you plan to spend time each day meditating on God's Word?

4. How can you help someone else who is stifled by fear?

Chapter Four

Take Calculated Risks

Trusting God's Sovereignty, Wisdom, and Power

> *We have no power to face this vast army that is attacking us.*
> *We do not know what to do, but our eyes are on you.*
>
> 2 CHRONICLES 20:12

> *Only those who risk going too far can*
> *possibly find out how far they can go.*
>
> T.S. ELIOT

When Linda accepted the invitation to become president and CEO of Sky Ranch in east Texas, one of the nation's largest Christian camps and conference centers, it was not exactly the direction she had planned for her life. Formerly the president and CEO of Snelling and Snelling Inc., one of the nation's largest staffing firms, Linda had her life settled in Dallas. Little did she know that the board at Sky Ranch camps had been praying diligently about their next leader and felt strongly that she was the perfect person for the position. After much wrestling in prayer and even saying no a couple of times, God made it clear to Linda that she was to accept the position. It was a step of faith and a change from what she was used to, but she ultimately knew she needed to be where God wanted her to be. Some may call it a risk, but Linda would call it trusting God.[1]

All of us face decisions in our lives, and often those decisions include risks. Risk that the job won't work out, risk that the house we just bought may have some issues, risk that the pregnancy may be difficult, risk that our children may give us discipline challenges, risk that the mastiff puppy we just bought may get too big (well, that's more of a fact than a risk)—but the point is, we face a myriad of unknowns every day. When we face a decision we must consider it with all wisdom and prayerfully seek God's direction. As we sense His leading, we move forward with courage and faith. We may face a few pitfalls, but that's part of the package of stepping forward and taking risks.

One of my favorite verses—one that I quote every morning—is Psalm 37:23-24. It is a beautiful reminder of God's care and provision through the risks of life. "The LORD directs the steps of the godly. He delights in every detail of their lives. Though they stumble, they will never fall, for He holds them by the hand" (NLT). There is no guarantee that every risk we take will be a great success, but there is a guarantee that as God directs our steps, He will hold us by the hand even when we stumble or fall. Risk-taking involves courage and the willingness to stumble and grow, leaning on Him each step of the way.

Rare and Wise

God accomplishes great things through those who are willing to be led by Him. Take Deborah, for example. Her story is found in the book of Judges in the Old Testament. Israel had been living in cycles: doing evil in the eyes of the Lord, being taken captive by an enemy, crying out to God for help, and then being rescued. In each cycle, God raised up a judge, a deliverer for His people. It is in the midst of one of the "captivity, cry out, get rescued" cycles that we see a surprising leader emerge. A woman! In a culture that was dominated by men, Deborah emerged as the leader of Israel. Judges 4 tells us she held court under the Palm of Deborah and the Israelites came to her to have their disputes decided. Clearly, we can see she was a wise and respected leader, who was using her gifts to advise, counsel, and mediate the disputes of the Israelites.

We also discover that she listened to God and obeyed Him, even when it involved taking risks. At the time she was a judge, Israel had fallen into the hands of Jabin, king of Canaan. The commander of his army, Sisera, had over 900 chariots. Like the army tanks of the ancient world, these chariots commanded respect, and the Israelites felt powerless against them. Yet, it was during this time that Deborah received a command from God to instruct an Israelite named Barak to prepare for battle. Unlike Moses, who argued with God, Deborah was willing to step forward and face her fear with faith in God's Word.

She sent for Barak and gave him this message: "The LORD, the God of Israel, commands you, 'Go take with you ten thousand men of Naphtali and Zebulun and lead them up to Mount Tabor. I will lead Sisera, the commander of Jabin's army, with his chariots and his troops to the Kishon River and give him into your hands.'"[2] God gave clear instructions and a promise of victory, but Barak responded by saying, "If you go with me, I will go; but if you don't go with me, I won't go."[3]

In my personal opinion, I think Deborah's greatest risk wasn't the preparation for battle, but rather sending Barak (Mr. Weak-Knees) as the army leader. Thank goodness I'm not in charge. God told Deborah to give the command to Barak, and she willingly and obediently did it, but she also gave Barak a consequence for his lack of faith.

She said, "Certainly I will go with you…But because of the course you are taking, the honor will not be yours, for the LORD will deliver Sisera into the hands of a woman."[4]

Bottom line: Deborah believed God, and Barak did not. Notice the contrast between a leader who was willing to step out of her comfort zone based on the Word of God, and another leader who played it safe and did not trust God's Word. God had clearly said that He would give Sisera into Barak's hands. Barak's job was to believe what God said was true, step forward, and take the risk. Barak's true character is revealed—he wasn't just fearful, he was faithless. His focus was on the big enemy army instead of the almighty God.

Here's how the battle is described in Judges, "At Barak's advance, the LORD routed Sisera and all his chariots and army by the sword, and Sisera got down from his chariot and fled on foot."[5] Did you read that? Barak advanced, yet God did the routing. It was God's battle the entire time; all Barak had to do was step forward based on God's direction. What seemed like a risk was actually a step of faith, based on what God said He would do.

And a woman did get the recognition! It wasn't Deborah, but another woman named Jael. As Sisera fled, he came to Jael's camp hoping to find refuge. Jael's husband had a friendly relationship with Jabin the king, so Sisera figured he could find help there. But Jael's loyalty was with Israel. She was not only brave, she was resourceful. Sisera asked for water, but she gave him milk. Warm milk made a wonderful bedtime snack and the exhausted Sisera went fast to sleep. At this point Jael made her move and drove a tent peg through his temple into the ground. Oh my! All that to say, the battle MVP award went to a woman.

Risk-Taker, Praise-Maker

Wouldn't it be fascinating if after every military battle, the victorious military leaders sang a little victory ballad or gave an after-battle concert? Picture Churchill and Truman singing a delightful duet. Or Patton and Eisenhower belting out a little battle-victory ditty. Actually, it wouldn't be the first time something crazy like that happened. Take the unlikely duo of Deborah and Barak, who sang a song on the day of their battle to recap the events, blow by blow. They offer the battle details in poetic form. I wonder what tune it was sung to—maybe something like the theme song to *Star Wars* or *Rocky*. Here are the opening lines of the song, which is found in Judges 5:

> When the princes in Israel take the lead,
>> when the people willingly offer themselves—
>> praise the Lord!
>
> Hear this, you kings! Listen, you rulers!
>> I, even I, will sing to the LORD;
>> I will praise the LORD, the God of Israel, in song.
>
> When you, LORD, went out from Seir,
>> when you marched from the land of Edom,
> the earth shook, the heavens poured,
>> the clouds poured down water.
> The mountains quaked before the LORD, the One of
>>   Sinai,
>> before the LORD, the God of Israel.
>
> In the days of Shamgar son of Anath,
>> in the days of Jael, the highways were abandoned;
>> travelers took to winding paths.

Villagers in Israel would not fight;
    they held back until I, Deborah, arose,
    until I arose, a mother in Israel.

God chose new leaders
    when war came to the city gates,
but not a shield or spear was seen
    among forty thousand in Israel.
My heart is with Israel's princes,
    with the willing volunteers among the people.
    Praise the LORD![6]

As you can see, Deborah's and Barak's hearts are filled with praise toward God because they recognized the victory came from Him. What a beautiful reminder to praise God in all things, but especially to remember to praise Him and thank Him for the victories in our lives! It's easy to get caught up in the thrill of victory or the glory of the moment, but we sometimes fail to remember to whom the thanksgiving and praise is due. Why is this so important? When we turn and recognize that it was God that did the work, we put pride in its place. Instead of becoming arrogant and diminishing our need for God, praise helps us remain humble and turns our eyes back to our provider and helper. When we turn our hearts upward, we acknowledge that our strength comes from Him.

By singing God's praises, the people of Israel had an opportunity to retell the story of all He had done for them. They could help their children and others understand His goodness and rejoice in His faithfulness. As a leader, whether in your home, your church, or your community, never fail to retell the stories of God's greatness. A godly leader is not only a risk-taker, but also a praise-maker. Let us give glory and honor where it is due so we do not allow ourselves to become complacent or self-sufficient or arrogant.

Several years ago a dear friend of mine invited me to come and encourage the women at her church. Her husband, who was the pastor of the church, prayed with us before the event began. And what a glorious prayer it was, giving the day over to God and seeking His blessing. I can testify that God moved in a powerful way and spoke words of life-giving truth into the women who were there. I knew it was God's power and love pouring through me without a doubt. The reason I am mentioning this gathering is not because of what happened during the event, but rather what happened afterward. When most of the people had gone home, the pastor and my friend came back in and prayed with me again, this time thanking and praising God for what He had done that day.

Oddly, as long as I have been speaking, I can rarely remember a time when the event planners and I deliberately stopped to pray and thank God after the event. There is usually so much to do—cleanup, evaluations, putting chairs back where they belong. But we should never be too busy to praise the Lord for His work. Let us take a cue from my friend, as well as from Deborah and Barak, and intentionally take time to praise God for the work He has done and will continue to do. Even if you don't see the fruit of your labor yet, trust Him that seeds were planted that will bear fruit as you abide with Him.

A risk-taker is a praise-maker. Why? Because a risk-taker steps out in faith and shows how big God is. A risk-taker is wise, but doesn't remain boxed into only what is safe and predictable. A risk-taker seeks God's direction and obeys even when it doesn't all make sense. A risk-taker believes in a big God to do big things. A risk-taker recognizes that it is He who leads and provides. A risk-taker praises God so others may see His goodness and rejoice.

Prayer Risk

There are times when the riskiest thing we can do is pray and leave the results up to God. Praying is risky in human terms, because it is stepping out in faith and leaning in on God to accomplish far more than we could accomplish on our own. Prayer is an everyday risk. A person who devotes an hour (or hours) of the early morning to prayer is taking a risk—a risk that the hour could have been spent sleeping, working, striving, or trying to make things happen on their own. Martin Luther said, "I have so much to do that I shall spend the first three hours in prayer." Now that's a risk-taker and a praise-maker. Luther had such strong faith in a great God who desires to answer prayer that he risked three hours of his busy day on his knees!

When I look at Deborah's faith and her ability to lead, it seems to stem from an intimate relationship with God. She heard Him. She recognized His voice. He told her to go into battle, and He told her how to do it. We don't know exactly how He spoke to Deborah, but we do know that she listened to Him. Her risk was not based on her own crazy ideas. The risk she took was based on the very words of God. There are a lot of crazy opportunities in our world to take big risks, but let us be wise and move on the foundation of God's Word as well as looking to Him for direction.

A friend of mine struggled with some family members and their unwise choices. She wanted to fix them and change them, but she also realized her limitations to do so. As she prayed about the issues, she began to realize she was powerless to make a difference in her family member's lives. She also realized that although she was power-less, God was powerful and able to do what she could not do. Instead of trying to fix the broken parts of their lives, she took the risk of pulling her hands off the situation and instead putting her hands together in prayer. She prayed consistently and emphatically that God would do the work and fight the battle.

When we decide to take our needs to God and leave them in His hands, we are becoming a prayer-warrior and risk-taker. We begin trusting God rather than ourselves. Sometimes He may lead us to take action, as He did with Deborah and Barak, and sometimes He may lead us to wait and let Him do the work. Most important, let us remember that our greatest action happens as we are on our knees.

The final verse in Barak's and Deborah's song is, "So may all your enemies perish, LORD! But may all who love you be like the sun when it rises in its strength."[7] Fellow leader, my prayer for you is that your love for God will be so strong that you will continually walk in His ways and His wisdom as you serve others, and thoughtfully step forward in faith. May you be like the sun that rises in its strength with boldness and clarity, lighting the way for those who follow.

=========== *Positive Leadership Strategy* ===========

POWERFUL TRUTH

Be willing to take risks—not recklessly—but with wisdom and a God-confidence.

PLAN OF ACTION

Be wise and discerning.

Seek God's leadership, guidance, and direction.

Step out in faith and obedience, even when it doesn't make sense.

Be brave and be resourceful with what God has given you.

Give praise to God for who He is and the work that He is doing.

Make prayer your most important action of the day.

Practice It

1. Describe a time you stepped out and took a risk.

2. How do prayer and praise strengthen you as a leader?

3. What does taking a calculated risk do for your faith, as well as the faith of others?

Chapter Five

Learn from Your Mistakes

Making the Best out of Your Worst

Praise the LORD, my soul,
and forget not all his benefits—
… who redeems your life from the pit
and crowns you with love and compassion.

PSALM 103:2,4

We should consider it pure joy when faced
with temptations of many kinds because God can use
those very experiences to purify us.
Do you believe there is anything Satan
devises that can outwit God?

JENNIFER KENNEDY DEAN

When we walk in a room and switch on a light, we can be thankful for an unlikely genius named Thomas Alva Edison. Moving pictures and audio recordings are also a result of this one man's perseverance. Few people expected young Thomas to amount to anything at all. But…he had a mother who looked past his shortcomings and saw his potential. He spoke with affection about her: "My mother was the making of me. She was so true, so sure of me; and I felt I had something to live for, someone I must not disappoint."

Thomas was a curious boy and his mother, Nancy, had every

reason to be discouraged about his actions. He burned down the family stable and was kicked out of school, yet his mother, a devout Presbyterian with a formal education, was able to put her education to good use by teaching "young Al." Thomas was an ambitious entrepreneur and started a small business selling newspapers on a local train, but he lost his job because he nearly blew up one of the train cars with his science experiments. His life was marked by many other failures and mishaps as well, but oddly that's not what we remember about him. We remember him for his successes. Aren't you thankful for the influence and leadership of his mother, who taught him to look at each failure as an opportunity to learn and grow and discover new things?

Edison had a unique drive and perseverance that kept him learning and growing despite his mistakes. He didn't allow discouragements to linger; rather he pushed forward with curiosity and commitment. On the fiftieth anniversary of the invention of the electric lightbulb, Henry Ford organized a celebration of his dear friend Edison. President Herbert Hoover spoke about the variety of ways that the electric light had made life better: "It enables our towns and cities to clothe themselves in gaiety by night, no matter how sad their appearance may be by day. And by all its multiple uses it has lengthened the hours of our active lives, decreased our fears, replaced the dark with good cheer, increased our safety, decreased our toil, and enabled us to read the type in the telephone book."[1]

The lightbulb represents countless hours in the laboratory filled with failed experiments and frustrations. When asked by a reporter with the *New York Times* about the seemingly incredible difficulties associated with developing his device, Edison responded, "I have not failed 700 times. I've succeeded in proving 700 ways how not to build a light bulb." What an extraordinary perspective! Can we look at our mistakes as successes, or are we so caught up in the disappointments and frustrations that we can't see the positive aspects of our failures? As leaders, let's determine to look at life with an attitude that includes the joy of learning and the opportunity to discover the lesson behind each challenge and mistake.

Odd Choice

If I were going to choose the recipient of the "Man After God's Own Heart" award, I would probably give it to someone like Elijah or Daniel or Joshua or even Enoch. These men didn't have a lot of screwups in their lives (at least that we know about) and they seemed to live in close relationship to God. Oddly, however, God chose to give the award to a man who lied, murdered, committed adultery, and caused the death of many others.

Hmm...seems like a strange choice doesn't it? But sometimes those people who seem like the biggest failures are also the ones who offer the greatest success stories. If we focus on David's shortcomings in the Old Testament, we can easily become disgusted by his actions, but here we find a man who did not allow the disappointments to keep him from being all that God had created him to be. David was a giant-slaying, praise-singing, big-hearted king who was one of the greatest leaders in the Old Testament, and of course in the lineage of Jesus.

What leadership skills can we learn from his ability to bounce back after trials? Let's take a brief look at his life story. He was a shepherd, the youngest son of Jesse, and not necessarily respected by his older brothers. He obviously was a learner because at a young age we know he learned how to protect his sheep from lions and bears using only a slingshot. David also learned about the Lord as he sat underneath the stars at night; he learned to rely on God as his refuge and his strength. When David saw that the Israelites were being taunted by a Philistine giant named Goliath, he drew upon what he had learned from the challenges in the wilderness. His faith in a big God and his ability to use a sling proved fatal to the Philistine giant.

After David slew the giant, his problems were just beginning. Israel's king, Saul, became jealous of David's fame and popularity. David soon became a fugitive running from Saul and his army. One particular story is found in 1 Samuel 21. David fled to the town of Nob, where a priest named Ahimelech was located. David asked the priest for provisions and for his famous sword, Goliath's sword, which David had used to behead the giant after he fell. Ahimelech was a little disturbed that David was there alone and started asking questions. David responded deceitfully, telling Ahimelech that he was on a secret mission for the king. Unfortunately, Saul's servant happened to be there and eventually told the king. As a result, Saul went to Nob and had all 85 priests there, including Ahimelech, killed!

What a mess! What a mistake! What a terrible outcome! How did David respond when he heard the news? First, he took responsibility. "I am responsible for the death of your father's whole family," he said to Ahimelech's son, the lone survivor of the tragedy. He also told him to stay with him and he would protect him. David took responsibility with his words and his actions. As a leader, it is difficult to take responsibility, especially when others are hurt by our mistake.

It would have been easy for David to put all the blame on Saul and walk away absolving himself of guilt, but David knew his actions were partly to blame for this tragedy. If he had sought God for direction and told the truth to Ahimelech, perhaps the story would have turned out differently. Certainly Saul was the evil force in this terrible incident, but David recognized his part and took responsibility.

It appears that David began to realize the importance of seeking the Lord's direction first before taking action. Interestingly, in the very next passage (1 Samuel 23) we read the story of David fighting Israel's enemies, the Philistines. When David heard that the Philistines were looting a nearby city, he didn't just rush in and attack. Instead, he inquired of the Lord, asking Him if they should go and attack. God answered and told him to go and attack. David's men weren't feeling confident, so he inquired again. Again God answered him. Godly leaders seek God's direction first.

A Fatal Error

Fast-forward to David's reign. Saul was defeated and killed during a battle; David was crowned king and began to enjoy his accomplishments. Maybe he was getting a little too comfortable in his position as ruler over Israel. It was the time when kings went to war, but instead of leading his troops into battle, David chose to stay behind at the palace. Here is where he got into trouble. From the roof of his palace, he spied a beautiful neighbor, Bathsheba, bathing. David sent for her and took her to bed, and she became pregnant while her husband was at war. This looked bad, so David, being the responsible leader that he was, called for her husband to come home to sleep with his own wife.

Just a side note on Bathsheba's husband. His name was Uriah the Hittite. We read in Scripture that David had more than 30 "mighty men," who surrounded him and fought valiantly for him.[2] Uriah was one of those men. He was a foreigner, and yet he was committed to serving David. More than that, Uriah was committed to serving and honoring God. When David brought him back from the battle lines, he refused to sleep with his wife, saying, "The ark and Israel and Judah are staying in tents…How could I go to my house to eat and drink and make love to my wife?"[3] So he slept on his mat among his master's servants and did not go home. Uriah was a noble man; quite a contrast to David in this story!

David became desperate to cover his sin with pregnant Bathsheba. And so he had Uriah (his faithful servant) placed on the front line of battle where he would be killed. We may try to hide our sin, but God is the God who sees all. God sent Nathan the prophet to confront David. He would experience severe and shameful consequences as the result of his sin. Yet through this sorrowful experience in his life, he came to recognize his desperate need for God's mercy, compassion, and forgiveness. He became humble and contrite before God. He was Israel's king, yet he was willing to be broken. He didn't take his sin lightly, but rather grieved deeply over it. Read what he wrote after he acknowledged his sin to Nathan.

> Have mercy on me, O God,
> according to your unfailing love;
> according to your great compassion
> blot out my transgressions.
> Wash away all my iniquity

and cleanse me from my sin.
For I know my transgressions,
and my sin is always before me.
Against you, you only, have I sinned
and done what is evil in your sight;
so you are right in your verdict
and justified when you judge…
Create in me a pure heart, O God,
and renew a steadfast spirit within me.
Do not cast me from your presence
or take your Holy Spirit from me.
Restore to me the joy of your salvation
and grant me a willing spirit, to sustain me.[4]

David did not stay in the pit of grief over his sin. He repented and turned and began to live in the joy and strength that forgiveness brings. Yes, there were severe consequences to his sin, but there was also restoration. He asked God to restore to him the joy of His salvation. The words *create, renew, restore* imply a fresh start and a moving forward. We all make mistakes, and we all sin. Thankfully, God does not abandon us or label us "useless." As we turn from our sin and commit ourselves to God, He will restore and renew us for His work.

David went on to lead his people and bring honor to God's name. Later in his life he prepared his son Solomon to build God's temple and lead the nation of Israel. Most important, Jesus Himself came through the lineage of David. David fell, yet he turned and learned. He couldn't change the past, but he could find his strength in the Lord for the future.

Bounce Back

Possibly the greatest lesson any leader can learn is discovered in the classroom of brokenness. For it is in this humble classroom that we recognize our complete and utter need for God. In our arrogance we may think we are His gift to others as a leader, but in our brokenness we recognize His gift to us of grace, mercy, and forgiveness. If Thomas Edison had allowed every failed experiment to set him back or each flawed business deal to destroy him, where would we be today? He would have quit as a young man when he was fired from his first job, and you might have been reading this book by candlelight!

We can live in the defeat of our mistakes, continually beating ourselves up for what we could have done or should have done. Or we can move forward, growing and learning from our mess ups. My friend and fellow author, Victorya Rogers, often says, "Your greatest challenge will be your greatest impact." Victorya speaks from her own personal story, as she waited for God to bring the right man into her life. She waited and waited and waited. When she was 34 years old she finally met and married the man of her dreams. But her greatest challenge became her greatest message. She went on to become a relationship coach and wrote several books on the topic of dating, including *The Automatic Second Date* and *Finding a Man Worth Keeping*. I just love the fact that Victorya spells her name with "Victory" at the center![5]

What about you? Are you allowing your challenges to be your enemy, or are you growing through them? It's a choice we choose and a perspective we pick. The "bounce-back" effect is contagious. When the people around us see our ability to work through the agony of defeat and bounce back from our frustrations or mistakes, they too will be inspired to persevere and not lose hope. We lead by principle, and we lead by example.

Thank God for your flaws and failures, for through them He expands your understanding and teaches you new and marvelous truths. Thank Him that He forgives, redeems, and resurrects. Thank Him that He never leaves you, even when you feel alone. David learned that sin often has terrible consequences, but even when we walk through the darkest valley, we do not need to be afraid, for our Shepherd is close beside us. His grace is bigger than our sin. His love is greater than our failures. We do not abuse His grace as an excuse to sin; rather, His kindness draws us continually closer to Him. He makes all things new and turns our mistakes into His victories.

===== *Positive Leadership Strategy* =====

Powerful Truth

Allow your mistakes to strengthen you, teach you, and turn you into a better leader.

Practical Applications

Admit when you have made a mistake and take responsibility for it.

Grieve it and leave it. Don't continue to replay your mistakes in your mind.

Seek God's direction first.

Turn from sin and live a life of moral purity.

Allow your setbacks to turn your focus back toward God's
   goodness.
Thank God for your mistakes and the opportunity to grow.
Look for new opportunities or ways to do things differently.
Write down the lessons you have learned.
Use what you have learned to help others.

Personalize It

1. What would you consider to be the biggest blunder or
   failure you have experienced in your life so far?

2. What are the lessons you have learned or can learn as a
   result of this frustration? In what ways can you thank
   God for this situation?

3. Is there someone you can reach out to and encourage
   who has experienced a setback?

Chapter Six

Inspire Passion

Motivating the Hearts of Others

*We do not lose heart. Though outwardly
we are wasting away,
yet inwardly we are being renewed day by day.*

2 Corinthians 4:16-17

*The secret of power and of being in the
will of God was not something
that I had to sweat and strain for; it was, rather,
what I had to recognize as already present in my life.
God's will is God Himself, and that is my power.*

Henrietta Mears

Over the years, I've become fairly perceptive at recognizing qualities that make a poor leader. It's probably because I've placed one too many people in leadership positions and later realized they were doing more harm than good. Thankfully we can learn and grow from our mistakes. Here's my short list of characteristics of a not-so-great leader. Generally speaking it's not a good idea to choose a person for leadership who

- tends to gossip or look down on others.

- complains rather than finds solutions.

- has no initiative and can't make decisions.

- doesn't work well with people.

- is a discourager rather than an encourager.

- is self-centered or greedy or doesn't care about the needs of others.

- is constantly wondering what people think about them.

- has an aversion to hard work and serving others.

- lacks determination and drive.

What would you add to the list? It's easy to think up a list of negative qualities born out of our own experiences, but it takes a little more thought and insight to come up with a list of positive leadership qualities. One characteristic that seems to surface in great leaders is their ability to motivate others. For some, this intangible ability to inspire and influence seems to come naturally, while other leaders discover their ability to impassion people through the school of hard knocks. As we learned in the last chapter, difficulties and struggles can be the best instructor to mold us into powerfully inspiring leaders.

How can we unleash our inner influence and ability to inspire? There is one surprising leader in the Bible who provides that potent picture of the power to influence. He was humble, yet a visionary. He worked as if everything depended on him, but he prayed as though everything depended on God. He had faithful people working for him, but he also had spiteful enemies working against him. Nehemiah went from cupbearer in the service of the Persian king to city-builder for the King of kings. Let's discover the key to his success.

Moving Others into Action

In his book *Visioneering*, Andy Stanley described Nehemiah this way, "He was just a regular guy who caught a divine glimpse of what could and should be. And then went after it with all his heart."[1] It's difficult to pare down Nehemiah's powerful story to fit in this one little chapter, but I will attempt to give you the highlights of his passionate life.

When you open up the book of Nehemiah in the Old Testament you find the majority of Israelites in captivity. The story begins with Nehemiah chatting with several fellow Jews who reported that the walls and gates of Jerusalem were in horrible disrepair. Now to us that may seem like a "who cares" news story, but we must remember that Jerusalem was the Jews' holy city and represented the Jewish national identity. This was the place where the glory of the Lord's presence resided in the temple. It was shameful that the city walls had fallen into ruin, and the few Jews who were still in the city were unorganized and ineffective in rebuilding. They needed a strong leader to pull them together.

Nehemiah was deeply grieved by the state of affairs in Jerusalem, but what could he possibly do? He was just one man serving as the cupbearer for the Persian king. What could he do? He could pray, and that's exactly where he began. He mourned, he fasted, and he cried out to God. Notice the humility in his prayer:

> LORD, the God of heaven, the great and awesome God, who keeps his covenant of love with those who love him and keep his commandments, let your ear be attentive and your eyes open to hear the prayer your servant is praying before you day and night for your

servants, the people of Israel. I confess the sins we Israelites, including myself and my father's family, have
committed against you. We have acted very wick-
edly toward you. We have not obeyed the commands,
decrees and laws you gave your servant Moses…

Lord, let your ear be attentive to the prayer of this
your servant and to the prayer of your servants who
delight in revering your name. Give your servant success
today by granting him favor in the presence of this man.[2]

Nehemiah committed his concern to God, and God began to
act. The Persian king noticed Nehemiah's dejected countenance and
asked what the matter was. Nehemiah whispered a prayer and then
boldly asked the king if he could return to Jerusalem to help rebuild
it. I love how Nehemiah described the king's response. He wrote,
"Because the gracious hand of my God was on me, the king granted
my requests."[3]

Nehemiah knew he was not alone. He had a sense of God's presence throughout his life. At every twist and turn, he prayed. He knew
what he wanted, and he knew who to go to in order to get it. Passion
and prayer, passion and prayer—these words typify Nehemiah's journey. When he returned to Jerusalem, he began organizing the people,
assigning them specific jobs and locations along the wall. He put the
right people in the right positions to get the job done.

God's work is rarely done without opposition. Two ringleaders
arose, Sanballat and Tobiah, who did their best to discourage and
disrupt the rebuilding efforts. I like what actor Chuck Norris is said
to have remarked about obstacles: "I've always found that anything
worth achieving will always have obstacles in the way and you've got

to have that drive and determination to overcome those obstacles en route to whatever it is that you want to accomplish." I think Chuck and Nehemiah could have been friends.

The Jewish workers grew weary and fearful as a result of their enemies' insults and threats. What would you do if you were Nehemiah? What would you do if you were Chuck Norris? Well, let's consider what Nehemiah did. Here's what he wrote:

> But we prayed to our God and posted a guard day and night to meet this threat...I stationed some of the people behind the lowest points of the wall at the exposed places, posting them by families, with their swords, spears, and bows. After I looked things over, I stood up and said to the nobles, the officials and the rest of the people, "Don't be afraid of them. Remember the Lord, who is great and awesome, and fight for your families, your sons and your daughters, your wives and your homes."[4]

Nehemiah always prayed in the face of obstacles. He was practical, purposeful, and prayerful. The thing I like about Nehemiah is that he had a prayerful plan, he put people in place, and he pointed people to God. The Bible tells us that the workers carried their building materials in one hand and their swords in the other. With a clear vision of what he wanted to accomplish, Nehemiah didn't allow distractions to get in the way. He pressed on, and he motivated the people to do the same. Do you know that the wall was completed in 52 days? That's unbelievable! That's the work of God. Almighty God loves to do what seems to us to be impossible.

Nehemiah did not try to build the wall himself. He empowered the people to build it. Notice I used the word *empowered* rather than *delegated*. It's one thing to delegate responsibilities to people, and it's another thing to empower them to take responsibility. He didn't just tell them what to do, he gave them the tools to do it, and then he motivated them to do it well. As a leader, we must be more than delegators; we must be empowerers, helping others to step up to their responsibilities. It may mean that we need to take the time to train and prepare people effectively, but in the long run we want to teach people how to fish, not simply give them fish.

Passionate Leader

Nehemiah faced his challenges head on. Despite insults and ridicule, he kept his fellow Jews on task. He not only dealt with discouragement, but he also cleaned house. Sadly, just as there were challenges on the outside, there were some internal struggles as well. Fellow Jews were trying to profit from the plight of those who were working tirelessly to rebuild the wall, charging outrageous fees to their fellow countrymen when they needed to borrow money. Nehemiah put an immediate stop to their greed by making the extortionists pay back all that they took plus the usury. He also dealt severely with those who went against God's laws and married foreign wives. He was not only a man of passion; he was a man of conviction.

As I read the story of Nehemiah, several themes continue to surface again and again. These seem to be the key to his inspiring leadership abilities. I would encourage you as a leader to read the story of Nehemiah and glean the powerful lessons for yourself. Here are the principles I glean from his example:

- He possessed a heartfelt passion.

- He prayed for God's direction throughout every twist and turn.

- He was committed to the mission and determined to see it through.

- He was persistent despite the challenges.

- He held unswervingly to God's Word.

- He sincerely cared about the protection and well-being of the people.

- He appealed to people's hearts and core motivation, not just the external.

- He put the right people in the right positions, using their gifts and talents.

- He wasn't swayed by the opposition or people's opinions.

- He empowered the people to do their jobs well.

Nehemiah's passion to repair the walls of Jerusalem was personal. It came from the core of his very being. He loved the Lord with all his heart, and therefore wanted God's holy city to be restored. How do we motivate others? It begins by being personally motivated ourselves. If we aren't convinced that our cause is worthwhile, we can't convince others.

Therefore, it's good to do a motive check. Why do I want this position of leadership? Is it for my own personal glory, or is it for the good of others and the glory of God? Do I believe wholeheartedly in the mission? Nehemiah began his journey in humble prayer. Let us do the same.

Father, create in me a clean heart and renew a right spirit in me. Purge me from impure motives and help me to move forward with passion and purpose. Lead me every step of the way, for Your glory, in the power of Your spirit, and in Jesus' name, Amen.

A Burning Passion

Like Nehemiah, my friend Becky didn't plan to rise to the place of leadership in her community, but her personal passion (the one God put in her heart) led her to places she never thought she would go. It became a journey of faith and a walk of prayer. I'll let her tell you her own story:

> I've often heard it said that God does not call the equipped, He equips the called. He started preparing my heart for the ministry He was calling to me nine months before I had a clue what He was up to.
>
> God gave me a burning passion for corporate prayer. As I caught a glimpse of what He does when His people humbly come before Him and pray, my excitement and desire to spend time with others in His presence grew. I realized that we do not ask Him for nearly enough; in the words of C.S. Lewis, "Our Lord finds our desires not too strong, but too weak…We are far too easily pleased." I wanted to start asking God for bigger things so that He might receive the glory.
>
> I waited many months before I realized why God had placed this desire for corporate prayer within me. During the waiting period, I agreed to serve at my

daughter's school by leading prayer meetings for her class. Somehow I didn't make the connection between serving in this capacity and the passion for corporate prayer!

As I sat in the training meeting for prayer leaders, God made the connection in my mind and it jolted me like a lightning bolt! I realized what He was doing! I pressed into Him like never before, seeking His will in leading moms to pray. He flooded my mind with ideas: ideas for our meetings, ideas for ministering, and ideas for leading the entire prayer ministry at the school. My mind overflowed with these God-ideas so much that I was forced to sit down at my computer and just type in order to get the ideas out of my head. One document I typed before I led even a single grade-level prayer meeting was titled, "If I were prayer coordinator *coordinator*." The Lord flooded my heart with His heart for this ministry at the school.

I am not a natural leader; I usually prefer to follow. However, when the Lord gives you a passion for something and you're following Him, leading others becomes easy and natural. I continued to pray about leading in the prayer ministry at our kids' school, but at the time there was no overall leader. God works in amazing ways, because halfway through the school year a new position was created for two "prayer coordinator coordinators"! When I was asked if I would consider taking on this role, I immediately said yes because I had already been praying about it. What a joy and a privilege to serve in the place God has called me to![5]

Perhaps, like Becky and Nehemiah, God has placed a passion

---

for His purpose deep inside your heart. Continue to take it to Him in prayer and seek His direction. He will open the doors for you to walk through and do a mighty work through you. He will give you what it takes to lead, despite the difficulties and challenges along the way. The beautiful message we learn from Nehemiah is that each struggle brings us back to our knees saying, as he did, "But I prayed." May prayer be our constant theme as we serve Christ according to our passion.

Positive Leadership Strategy

Powerful Truth

Inspirational leaders are motivated by an authentic passion at their core which allows them to inspire others.

Practical Applications

Recognize what motivates you.

Use each challenge to teach you and build you into a better leader.

Pray about everything, seeking God's direction at every turn.

Place the right people in the right positions.

Persevere despite opposition and obstacles.

Deal decisively with people and situations that are divisive.

Don't let your enemies discourage you.

Be practical as well as prayerful.

Empower others with responsibility.

Personalize It

1. What are some current issues you are passionate about right now?

2. What is a practical first step you can take in leading the cause and making a difference?

3. Which of the principles from Nehemiah's example do you plan to apply in your leadership role?

Chapter Seven

Choose to Do the Tough Stuff

Serving with Strength and Humility

Do not conform to the pattern of this world,
but be transformed by the renewing of your mind.
Then you will be able to test and
approve what God's will is—
His good, pleasing and perfect will.

ROMANS 12:2

My brokenness is a better bridge for people
than my pretend wholeness ever was.

SHEILA WALSH

Thelma Wells is known for her smile, her candor, and her hope-infused messages to women. She was one of the first black women executives in the banking industry; in the following years she has become known worldwide as a Woman of Faith speaker, conference leader, and popular author. But her life hasn't always been an easy road to success. Her mother was an unwed teenager in a day when it was considered shameful to be pregnant and not married. Her maternal grandmother would not allow Thelma and her mom to stay in her home, so they lived in servants' quarters in a house in Dallas.

Thelma remembers visiting her grandmother's home as a little girl and being put in the closet—a dark, dingy, insect-infested closet—yet it was here that she began to sing the songs she remembered from church. Songs like "Amazing Grace" and "The Old Rugged Cross." Here in this dark dungeon, she felt a closeness to God. She said, "I would sing myself to sleep with church songs. I had no bitterness, no anger, no strife, no malice, and no fear." What a picture of God hiding His children under the shadow of His wings!

Years later, Thelma ended up taking care of that very same elderly grandmother for 13 years. Although her grandmother never said, "I'm sorry" or "I love you," by God's grace Thelma was able to forgive her in her heart. There have been other trials along Thelma's journey, like the time she almost died from what she thought was a routine hysterectomy. When the doctors began surgery they found cancer. In a second surgery her lungs collapsed and she nearly lost her life. She's faced heartaches personally and even walked through depression, but through the pain her message has never wavered. She continues to proclaim God's faithfulness and the hope we find in Him.

Thelma says, "God does not always heal us instantly the way we think. He is not a jack-in-the-box God. But God is walking with me through this. As I keep singing a song in my heart, every day I get up with peace and hope and love and joy because I know it could be so much worse."[1]

Leader's Life

A leader's life is not always glamorous. In fact, a godly leader may find her life riddled with trials, loneliness, and even sadness at times. Jeremiah was a lonely leader. We could label him "Mr. Unpopular" or "The Prophet No One Would Listen To." He actually is known as the "Weeping Prophet." He wrote Lamentations, which is not exactly the feel-good book of the year! His life was no joyride; he was rejected, thrown into prison, put down into a muddy pit, kidnapped, and despised. His message of repentance seemed to fall on deaf ears. He stood alone, but he stood on the foundation of God's Word.

Unlike Nehemiah, who developed leadership skills as a result of his struggles, Jeremiah was a born leader. God told Jeremiah, "Before I formed you in the womb I knew you, before you were born I set you apart; I appoint you as a prophet to the nations." [2] Now just because God had prepared him to be a leader in his mother's womb, that didn't mean Jeremiah felt equipped for the task. He responded, "Alas, Sovereign LORD, I do not know how to speak; I am too young." [3] Does that remind you of another leader we know? Ahem...Moses. I'm reminded of the great little maxim my friend Becky mentioned in the previous chapter: "God does not call the equipped, He equips the called."

Here's how the Lord responded to Jeremiah: "Do not say, 'I am too young.' You must go to everyone I send you to and say whatever I command you. Do not be afraid of them, for I am with you and will rescue you." [4] Wow, I've heard those words before—*do not be afraid, for I am with you!* Doesn't that seem to be the same message God gave to each leader we have studied? In what area do you feel fearful or ill-equipped as a leader? Hear God's message—"Do not be afraid, I am with you." What comfort we find from those words!

Jeremiah continued to write about his encounter with God: "Then the LORD reached out his hand and touched my mouth and said to me, 'I have put my words in your mouth. See, today I appoint you over nations and kingdoms to uproot and tear down, to destroy and overthrow, to build and to plant.'"[5] Looks like Jeremiah was in for an interesting journey! No smooth, direct route here! Just because God calls us and directs us doesn't mean our mission will be smooth sailing all the way. Jeremiah's life is a testimony of difficult travels. I'm reminded of Paul, who experienced similar challenges in his work for the Lord. Paul wrote, "We have this treasure in jars of clay to show that this all-surpassing power is from God and not from us. We are hard pressed on every side, but not crushed; perplexed, but not in despair; persecuted, but not abandoned; struck down, but not destroyed."[6]

Our struggles do not necessarily mean we are off base or haven't heard from the Lord. This is important for us to note as leaders. Even when we are going in the direction God has given us, there are no guarantees we will have a stress-free journey. Don't be discouraged if you face frustrations, hurts, loneliness, or setbacks. Sometimes God uses these difficult times to refine us, to teach us, to grow us up. Other times, the difficulties we experience can be used to comfort others and help them through rough spots. We learn from Jeremiah's story that disappointments and discouragements do not mean failure. Remember, successful leadership in God's eyes is defined as doing what we know He has called us to do, despite the difficulties or loneliness.

The Truth Isn't Always Popular

Jeremiah was called to bring a message of doom to the Israelites, so you can imagine he wasn't considered the "life of the party." He called the people of Judah to repentance because they had wandered far from God. During this time, the people of Judah rejected the Lord and strayed toward idols (again), and lived largely in personal unrighteousness. Sadly, they refused to listen to Jeremiah's message of repentance. In fact one king, Jehoiakim, hated Jeremiah's written message so much that he cut it up and threw it into the fire. Yes, this prophet definitely was not an ear-tickler.

It was Jeremiah's job not only to preach repentance, but also to foretell Judah's destruction. It's interesting that a well-loved passage in Jeremiah is actually part of his warning. Perhaps you are familiar with the encouraging words found in Jeremiah 29:11: "'I know the plans I have for you,' declares the LORD, 'plans to prosper you and not to harm you, plans to give you hope and a future.'"

This verse is used in many a sermon as a reassurance that God has great and successful plans for us. It makes you think that He intends for our lives to be happy, smooth, and prosperous, but if we read the passage as a whole we see that God is giving a message to His people who are exiled in Babylon. It is a message to let them know that they are going to be there in exile for 70 years. The message is one of perseverance and hope, but the most important part of the message is that they must keep their eyes on the Lord. The rest of the passage is this:

> "Then you will call on me and come and pray to me, and I will listen to you. You will seek me and find me when you seek me with all your heart. I will be found by you," declares the LORD, "and will bring you back from captivity. I will gather you from all the nations and places where I have banished you," declares the Lord, "and will bring you back to the place from which I carried you into exile."[7]

God's invitation was and always will be, "Turn your eyes on Me, look to Me, I am your Redeemer." God has good plans for us, but it may mean a time of waiting and persevering. In Judah's case, the wait was 70 years. Jeremiah faced a tough ministry that seemed to go from bad to worse. When we find ourselves in the midst of discouragement or when we are tempted to despair, remember God's message of hope to the exiled. He has great plans for you. You are not alone. He can use even the worst of circumstances for a beautiful and bigger plan.

Faith Built in Darkness

"In the northwest corner of Harvard Yard stands a building as massive as the man whose name it bears. At six feet, four inches and nearly three hundred pounds, Phillips Brooks, A.B. 1855, S.T.D. 1877, was an outstanding figure of Harvard's Victorian age," reads *Harvard Magazine*. It goes on to say,

> What was the secret of this man's remarkable life and influence? Brooks wrote in 1891, "...These last years have had a peace and fullness which there did not use to be. I am sure that it is not indifference to anything I used to care for. I am sure that it is a deeper knowledge and truer love of Christ...I cannot tell you how personal this grows to me. He is here. He knows me and I know Him. It is no figure of speech. It is the realest thing in the world. And every day makes it realer."[8]

A pensive clergyman and author, Brooks experienced a depth of faith through the struggles of life. He wrote,

I often hear people praying for more faith, but when I listen carefully to them and get to the essence of their prayer, I realize it is not more faith they are wanting at all. What they are wanting is their faith to be changed to sight. Faith does not say, "I see this good for me; therefore God must have sent it." Instead, faith declares, "God sent it; therefore it must be good for me." Faith, when walking through the dark with God, only asks Him to hold his hand more tightly.[9]

Isn't that an amazing perspective on faith? Even in the gloomiest moments of our lives, God does not leave us. When Jeremiah was at his lowest point, he was still able to rally his faith and find his hope in God. As leaders, we will face discouraging moments especially as we stand up for what is right. But even though Jeremiah faced rock bottom, he knew he could look up and find his hope in the Lord. He waited on Him through the troubling times. In the book of Lamentations, Jeremiah wrote a powerful commentary of hope rising up from despair:

> I remember my affliction and my wandering,
>   the bitterness and the gall.
> I well remember them,
>   and my soul is downcast within me.
> Yet this I call to mind
>   and therefore I have hope:
> Because of the LORD's great love we are not consumed,
>   for his compassions never fail.
> They are new every morning;
>   great is your faithfulness.

> I say to myself, "The LORD is my portion;
> > therefore I will wait for him."
> The LORD is good to those whose hope is in him,
> > to the one who seeks him;
> it is good to wait quietly
> > for the salvation of the LORD.[10]

Allow Jeremiah's words to be your strength through troubling times. When you feel alone. When you feel like no one else is listening. When you feel like you have made a mistake. When you feel rejected by your own people…may Jeremiah's words be your comfort and reminder to keep your eyes on the Lord and wait patiently for Him. He does have a good plan. We may not see the fruit until we stand with Him in eternity, but let us remain faithful to the message He has given us no matter what the cost. Persevere in hope.

Be a "LeadHer"

When Christie found herself a newly single mother of three young children, she felt discouraged and disqualified from ministry due to her failed marriage. In an attempt to rekindle her hope and faith, she went to a weekend women's conference with friends and family. She enjoyed the conference and the chance to connect with women of different ages, backgrounds, and professions. Though they were all different, they were united by their faith in God and their passion for finding His purposes for their lives. As she sat in the audience, she could not help but think how the "spiritual high" she was experiencing was going to quickly fade when she returned home to her children, the cooking, and the dirty laundry that all demanded her attention and energy. Wishing there was a way to bottle the energy and encouragement of that weekend for continual use, Christie began to realize the great need for a way to unite women similarly in communities across the nation.

When she returned home, Christie began researching to see if a program existed that united women of faith from different ages, church affiliations, and professions. She could not find one. So she began to pray that God would send someone who was qualified and experienced in ministry to come alongside her. After several years of praying that prayer…she recognized God wasn't going to give this plan to someone else because He had entrusted her with it. She knew the calling He had placed on her life required her to be "all in" with Him.

Christie began praying for direction and wisdom. God began to bring together women with similar passions, skills, and a willingness to help her build this ministry from the ground up. LeadHer was officially launched on May 1, 2011, from Christie's home in southwest Missouri. Later that year, LeadHer published its first daily devotional book: *The LeadHer Challenge*, written by eight women who came together to create a unique resource to encourage, equip, and challenge women daily. LeadHer now has chapters around the country and even internationally, bringing women together and focusing on "growing women God's way in their own communities."[11]

Like Jeremiah, Christie stepped up and stepped into action, following God's call on her life to lead women. She did not stop and look back, saying, "This is too hard." Instead she stepped forward, looking to God to guide her day by day. We need leaders today who are not in it for their own glory, but rather to serve God and others. Let us be leaders who inspire a passion for God, who are willing to be "all in," and who make a positive difference in the lives of others.

Powerful Truth

Choose to do the tough stuff, maintaining an attitude of hope.

Practical Application

Listen to God and follow His call.

Point people to the Lord.

Don't be afraid or discouraged by rough roads.

Remember that our loving God has a good plan.

Always proclaim the hope God can bring to any situation.

Faith is strengthened as we walk through the darkness hand in hand with God.

Personalize It

1. What are some of the areas in your leadership where you may have to stand alone?

2. How have you experienced God's mercy and strength through tough times in the past?

3. What tough stands or unpopular issues you have been avoiding?

Chapter Eight

Know Where to Go for Help

Looking Up Before Looking Out

> *I lift up my eyes to the mountains—*
> *where does my help come from?*
> *My help comes from the LORD,*
> *the Maker of heaven and earth.*
>
> PSALM 121:1-2
>
> *I don't know how, but I know Who!*
>
> BETH MOORE

Recently I heard a summary of the results of a study by the Cato Institute, stating, "Poverty is perpetuated through poor parenting." That statement has stuck with me. I must admit, my heart has grieved for many years for "at-risk" kids who have little hope of breaking out of the cycle of poverty. As I began asking the Lord what I could do to make a difference, He flooded my mind with this thought: *Karol, you go all over the nation teaching men and women how to be positive parents—why aren't you going to the impoverished communities in your city?* As I considered what I felt God was leading me to, I didn't know how to start or what to do, so once again I asked Him to direct me.

When we look to God for wisdom, He is faithful to direct us! He led me to begin researching and seeking advice. I interviewed several friends who had grown up in poverty. The most important lesson I learned was to not go in with the attitude of "I'm going to fix you," but rather with an attitude of humility, recognizing that we all need fixing and only God can fix us.

With God leading me all along the way, I began to write out discussion-style lessons. The lessons enable parents to recognize their responsibility in their home and lead them to discover their own plans of action. With the concept in place, my next step was to figure out where to use it. Again, I didn't know where to go, so I asked the Lord to show me. Funny thing—I opened up the newspaper and saw an article about Buckner Children and Family Services of North Texas. Buckner had an outreach program in one of the housing developments in Dallas, so with a little bit of fear and trembling, I e-mailed them and asked if they were interested in any parenting classes.

They said yes! Oh my—now I had to take a step of faith and step out of my comfort zone and into the lives of men and women I had never met. I knew I didn't understand what their lives were like, but God did. So I prayed that He would love through me and make this a fruitful and meaningful time together with the parents. He answered that prayer! He has done an amazing work and has allowed me to build bridges through loving relationships with the parents in the community. I call the program ENGAGE Positive Parenting Initiative.

Even the name was a result of God's leading and direction. As I was praying for a name for the outreach, the word *engage* kept popping in my head. It made sense because the whole concept is to engage with parents and encourage them to engage in a positive way with their kids. One day I just thought, *Okay, I'll call it ENGAGE, but I wonder if that should stand for anything?* Immediately God flooded my mind (as He so faithfully does) with this acronym: "Equipping the Next Generation to Advance and Grow through Education, Encouragement, and Example." (Okay, so it is ENGAGEEE, but you get the point.)

From start to finish, God has directed me, and now He continues to open doors for me to take ENGAGE to other communities and cities.[1] Often I have felt like I don't have what it takes to start and lead this organization, but I know He will enable me to lead one step at a time. I feel as though I have just engaged (catch the pun) in battle, a battle for the family. It's time to build back the strength of the family in our nation. I feel like a woman on a mission!

Taking a Stand on His Knees

As leaders, there are times when we are called to courageously make a difference in our culture. When Daniel received the news of a new law in the land denying him his right to pray, he did not get angry. He did not begin a social-media campaign or organize a protest. He stood strong, or should I say, knelt strong. Here's how his story of strength started out. At the time, the Israelites were in exile and under foreign rule. Darius was king of the Medes, and Daniel was given a powerful place in leadership. We read in Daniel 6:

> It pleased Darius to appoint 120 satraps to rule throughout the kingdom, with three administrators over them, one of whom was Daniel. The satraps were made accountable to them so that the king might not suffer loss. Now Daniel so distinguished himself among the

administrators and the satraps by his exceptional qualities that the king planned to set him over the whole kingdom. At this, the administrators and the satraps tried to find grounds for charges against Daniel in his conduct of government affairs, but they were unable to do so. They could find no corruption in him, because he was trustworthy and neither corrupt nor negligent. Finally these men said, "We will never find any basis for charges against this man Daniel unless it has something to do with the law of his God."[2]

Did you notice that King Darius was ready to set Daniel over the whole kingdom? Daniel had risen to the top, and was considered the cream of the crop. Yet, jealousy set in among his enemies, and knowing Daniel's commitment to God, they created a plan. The conspirators went to the king with a devious idea. They presented it to Darius: "The royal administrators, prefects, satraps, advisers and governors have all agreed that the king should issue an edict and enforce the decree that anyone who prays to any god or human being during the next thirty days, except to you, Your Majesty, shall be thrown into the lions' den."[3]

Now if you were Daniel and had already been elevated as one of the highest administrators in the land, what would you have done? Take a moment to think about it—what would be your first response? What action would you have taken? Here's how Daniel responded: "Now when Daniel learned that the decree had been published, he went home to his upstairs room where the windows opened toward Jerusalem. Three times a day he got down on his knees and prayed, giving thanks to his God, just as he had done before."[4]

He prayed. And as we see throughout the book of Daniel, he prayed about everything and continually gave glory to God. He prayed about interpreting dreams. He prayed for his nation. Although he was one of the highest leaders in the land, he prayed with sincerity and humility. He was a leader who knew where his help came from. The secret to Daniel's ability to take a stand was his ability to take a knee—falling to his knees in prayer. Here is where he got his insight, his strength, his ability to lead. He got down on his knees three times a day, every day! Fellow leaders, how is your prayer life?

In the Den

It's hard to imagine what it was like during the night that Daniel spent in the den with the lions, but I can imagine it was an extraordinary experience. Here's what we do know: when King Darius ran to the den the next morning to see if he was alive, Daniel gave a short recap of the night: "My God sent his angel, and he shut the mouths of the lions. They have not hurt me, because I was found innocent in his sight. Nor have I ever done any wrong before you, Your Majesty."[5]

What a glorious night! Hungry lions, an angel, and Daniel. What a unique all-night prayer meeting! God brought the victory, and He received the glory. Daniel was courageous to take a stand, and yet he did it in a humble way; a way that depended on God and not himself. Notice the outcome. The king's heart was changed, and he gave honor and glory to God. Daniel's enemies were defeated.

> The king was overjoyed and gave orders to lift Daniel out of the den. And when Daniel was lifted from

the den, no wound was found on him, because he had trusted in his God.

At the king's command, the men who had falsely accused Daniel were brought in and thrown into the lions' den, along with their wives and children. And before they reached the floor of the den, the lions overpowered them and crushed all their bones.

Then King Darius wrote to all the nations and peoples of every language in all the earth:

"May you prosper greatly!

"I issue a decree that in every part of my kingdom people must fear and reverence the God of Daniel.

"For he is the living God
    and he endures forever;
his kingdom will not be destroyed,
    his dominion will never end.
He rescues and he saves;
    he performs signs and wonders
    in the heavens and on the earth.
He has rescued Daniel
    from the power of the lions."

So Daniel prospered during the reign of Darius and the reign of Cyrus the Persian.[6]

Daniel's loving stand for what was right pointed others to God. As salt and light in this world, our job is not to show how strong we are, but rather how great, powerful, and loving our God is. It is God who changes hearts, not us. He can use our stand to point people in His direction, so let us take a stand in love with the goal to point people to God's unfailing love.

In our current culture, we may be forced to take a stand on biblical values and our faith in Christ. Begin first on your knees. Humbly submit the situation to God, seeking His direction and guidance. Stand firm, be courageous, and remember the battle is the Lord's. Ask God to do the work. There may be times when we must move forward and there may be times when we need to quietly, lovingly stand our ground. If we humbly submit to God, He will give us wisdom and guidance.

Students Standing Strong

Strength comes through the humility of prayer. The writer of Hebrews reminds us of the strength that comes when we humble ourselves in prayer:

> Let us draw near to God with a sincere heart and with the full assurance that faith brings, having our hearts sprinkled to cleanse us from a guilty conscience and having our bodies washed with pure water. Let us hold unswervingly to the hope we profess, for he who promised is faithful. And let us consider how we may spur one another on toward love and good deeds, not giving up meeting together, as some are in the habit of doing, but encouraging one another—and all the more as you see the Day approaching.[7]

Don't you just love that word "unswervingly"? What about you? Are you holding unswervingly to the hope you profess? Daniel did.

And we can too, as we draw near to God and seek His help in the challenges we face.

All three of my college roommates are Daniel types. Julie rose to the top in leadership of Premiere Jewelry, a company based on biblical principles. Barbara became the head of the Texas State Board of Education, taking a stand for truth and values within the public-school systems. Terry Ann started a grassroots effort to encourage public-school students to take a stand (a Daniel-type stand) together for Christ. Her program is called Students Standing Strong.

Terry Ann's concept for Students Standing Strong started as a simple idea when her son was 11 years old. She wanted him to be equipped to face the challenges he would encounter as he entered middle school. Knowing that he would have choices to make regarding alcohol, drugs, and sexual promiscuity, she wanted him to be surrounded with like-minded friends, hoping that together they could stand strong against negative peer pressure. Terry Ann decided to simply invite every fifth grader in her son's public school to a party in the local park near her home. She planned to serve hot dogs and talk to them about how they could resist middle-school peer pressure by living according to God's Word.

As Terry Ann began to mention her idea to other parents it dawned on her that Catholic and Protestant parents all wanted the same thing. She said, "We all want our kids' faith to be so personal that it affects the way they live. We want our kids to not only have beliefs but to also have the conviction to live those beliefs out in their everyday life." As a result of that fifth-grade event, what began as a party has now grown into a ministry. Today, Students Standing Strong has spread to 26 schools—and that number is growing!

We need each other. Standing strong is better when we are standing together. Daniel had Shadrach, Meshach, and Abednego. I had my roommates in college. Terry Ann's kids have their friends in Students Standing Strong. Do you have people around you who will encourage you to stand strong? Let's be deliberate about surrounding ourselves with brothers and sisters who share our same convictions. On the other hand, even if we feel as though we stand alone, remember that as we stand on God's Word, He is right beside us. We can lean in hard on Him and trust His loving arms to hold us.

Where is God calling you to take a stand? Begin on your knees and allow Him to lead you. Think of the powerful impact we could have in our world if each of us reading this book courageously live out our convictions through our leadership positions! May the world be a different place as we stand strong, lead with love, and encourage one another.

Positive Leadership Strategy

POWERFUL TRUTH

Stand strong by recognizing that your help comes from the Lord.

PRACTICAL APPLICATIONS

Know what you believe and what is worth fighting for.
When called to take a stand, first go on your knees.
Ask God for courage to stand, even if everyone else is sitting.
Take action in love, not anger.

Find strength in the community of other believers.
Be an encourager to other leaders.

Personalize It

1. Which of your core beliefs are now being challenged in our culture?

2. Have you gone to your knees to pray about your stand?

3. How can we demonstrate Christ's love when we take a stand?

Eight Steps to Effective Leadership

Let your light shine before others, that
they may see your good deeds
and glorify your Father in heaven.

MATTHEW 5:16

We have walked together as we have examined the lives of eight leaders in the Bible. Now it's time for you to live out your leadership. One step at a time, begin walking forward using the gifts and talents God has given you. Be open to the plans He has for you—which may be slightly different than the plans you have had for yourself. Trust Him to light your path one step at a time. As you walk in fellowship with Him, He will shine His light through your words, actions, and example. As you courageously use the gifts and talents He has given you, our world will be a brighter place.

Here is a recap of the eight positive principles you learned in this book. Review them often and reflect on what God is teaching you about Himself through each of them.

1. Look at your mountains as opportunities for growth.

2. Focus on your strengths while managing around your weaknesses.

3. Be strong and courageous. Do not allow fear to grip your thinking.

4. Be willing to take risks using God's wisdom as your guide.

5. Learn from your mistakes instead of being discouraged by them.

6. Motivate others through passion, prayer, and practical plans.

7. Recognize that leadership can be lonely and difficult at times. Do not lose hope.

8. Find your strength and help in God to take a stand.

As a result of writing this book I decided to host quarterly Positive Leadership Lunches. Perhaps you want to do the same. Keep in touch and let's encourage each other to lead with a heart of service, keeping our eyes on the Lord. May the Lord shine brightly through you!

www.PositiveLifePrinciples.com

Recommended Reading for Leaders

Work hard and become a leader;
Be lazy and become a slave.

PROVERBS 12:24 NLT

Books are those faithful mirrors that
reflect to our mind the minds of sages and heroes.

GIBBON

Leaders are readers. I want to encourage you to read biographies as well as inspirational books to strengthen your effectiveness as a reader. Consider adding the following books to your leadership library.

50 People Every Christian Should Know by Warren Wiersbe (Baker Books)

Pray with Purpose, Live with Passion by Debbie Williams (Howard Books)

Spiritual Leadership by Oswald Sanders (Moody Publishers)

Visioneering by Andy Stanley (Multnomah)

They Found the Secret by V. Raymond Edman (Zondervan)

The Ten Best Decisions a Leader Can Make by Bill Farrel (Harvest House)

Successful Women Think Differently by Valorie Burton (Harvest House)

Notes

Never Underestimate the Power of a Woman's Influence

1. Zenger Folkman Co., "A Study in Leadership: Women Do It Better than Men," www.zfco.com/media/articles/ZFCo.WP.WomenBetterThanMen.031312.pdf.

Chapter 1—Rise to the Challenge

1. Genesis 39:2-6.

2. Genesis 39:8-9.

3. If you would like to know more about sponsoring a missionary with Gospel for Asia go to www.gfa.org.

4. Genesis 39:20-23.

5. Genesis 40:8.

6. Genesis 50:19-21.

7. C.H. Spurgeon, *Morning and Evening Daily Bible Readings* (Peabody, MA: Hendrickson, 1994), Morning March 7.

8. Mary Trotter Kion, www.historyswomen.com/1stWomen/MaryCrowley.html.

Chapter 2—Change Your Focus

1. Exodus 3:6.

2. Exodus 3:8.

3. Exodus. 3:14.

4. Exodus 4:1.

5. Exodus 4:10.

6. Exodus 4:11-12.

7. 2 Corinthians 12:7-10.

8. Exodus 4:13.

9. Exodus 4:14-17.

10. Numbers 12:3.

Chapter 3—Step Forward with Courage

1. *The Westminster Collection of Christian Quotes*, comp. Martin H. Manser (Louisville, KY: Westminster John Knox Press, 2001) p. 54.
2. Joshua 1:1-6.
3. Psalm 23:4.
4. Edmund Burke, *On the Sublime and Beautiful* (New York: Penguin Classics, 1999), p. 101.
5. Joshua 1:7-9.
6. Numbers 32:12.
7. Joshua 5:13-15; 6:2-5

Chapter 4—Take Calculated Risks

1. To find out more about Sky Ranch Christian camps go to www.skyranch.org.
2. Judges 4:6-7.
3. Judges 4:8.
4. Judges 4:9.
5. Judges 4:15.
6. Judges 5:2-9.
7. Judges 5:31.

Chapter 5—Learn from Your Mistakes

1. Herbert Hoover, "Address on the 50th Anniversary of Thomas Edison's Invention of the Incandescent Electric Lamp" (October 21, 1929).
2. 1 Samuel 23:39.
3. 2 Samuel 11:11.
4. Psalm 51:1-3,10-12.
5. To learn more about Victorya Rogers's books, go to www.Victorya.com.

Chapter 6—Inspire Passion

1. Andy Stanley, *Visioneering* (Colorado Springs, CO: Multnomah Books, 1999), p. 15.

2. Nehemiah 1:5-7,11.

3. Nehemiah 2:8.

4. Nehemiah 4:9,13-14.

5. Used by permission.

Chapter 7—Choose to Do the Tough Stuff

1. Thelma Wells, as interviewed by Sherry Huang, "Praising Behind Closed Doors," Beliefnet, www.beliefnet.com/Inspiration/Christian-Inspiration/2007/06/Praising-Behind-Closed-Doors.aspx?p=2.

2. Jeremiah 1:5.

3. Jeremiah 1:6.

4. Jeremiah 1:7.

5. Jeremiah 1:9.

6. 2 Corinthians 4:7-9.

7. Jeremiah 29:12-14.

8. Kay Peterson Hall, "Phillips Brooks: Brief Life of a Boston Minister: 1835-1893," *Harvard Magazine*, May 1996, www.Harvardmagazine.com/1996/05/vita.html.

9. Jim Reimann and L.B.E. Cowan, *Streams in the Desert* (Grand Rapids, MI: Zondervan, 2008), May 1 entry.

10. Lamentations 3:19-26.

11. For more information about Christie and LeadHer, go to www.LeadHer.org.

Chapter 8—Know Where to Go for Help

1. To find out more about ENGAGE Positive Parenting Initiative go to www.EngageParenting.com.

2. Daniel 6:1-5.

3. Daniel 6:7.

4. Daniel 6:10.

5. Daniel 10:22.

6. Daniel 6:23-28.`

7. Hebrews 10:22-25.

About the Author

Karol Ladd is known as "the Positive Lady." Her heart's desire is to inspire men and women with a message of lasting hope and biblical truth.

Karol is open, honest, and real in both her speaking and her writing. Formerly a teacher, she is the bestselling author of over 30 books, including *The Power of a Positive Mom, Thrive Don't Simply Survive,* and *A Woman's Passionate Pursuit of God.* As a gifted communicator and dynamic leader, Karol is a popular speaker for women's organizations, church groups, and corporate events across the nation. She is also a frequent guest on radio and television programs and teaches a monthly Bible study called Positive Woman Connection.

Karol devotes her time to several different ministries that encourage, strengthen, and help women around the world, including an organization she started called ENGAGE Positive Parenting Initiative. Her most valued role is that of wife and mother.

Visit her website at
www.PositiveLifePrinciples.com
Follow her on Twitter and Facebook too!

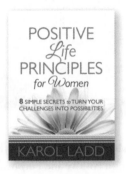
Positive Life Principles for Women
8 Simple Secrets to Turn Your Challenges into Possibilities

What woman doesn't sometimes feel like her life is "slightly imperfect"… maybe even over-the-top imperfect?

Bestselling author Karol Ladd looks at the not-so-perfect lives of eight women in the Bible to show you how to turn your challenges and blunders into possibilities for growth, change, and maturity. Eight powerfully effective chapters give you encouragement to

- *listen to the right voices*, shown by the life of Eve

- *guard against comparisons,* exemplified in the life of Sarah

- *reach out and help others,* demonstrated in the life of Ruth

You'll see how to learn from your mistakes and become stronger despite adversity…and find hope, refreshment, and renewal for your "slightly imperfect" life.

A Woman's Passionate Pursuit of God (book and DVD)
Creating a Positive and Purposeful Life

As you explore Paul's intriguing letter to the Philippians with popular author and speaker Karol Ladd, you'll learn to live intentionally as you face life's daily challenges. Most important, you'll be helped to understand God's Word and His plans for your life and say more and more, "Father, I want what You want."

Filled with inspiring true-life stories, practical steps, and study questions, this book is perfect for personal quiet times, a book club pick, or a group Bible study.

It's complemented by the DVD version, offering six 30-minute sessions from Karol, a helpful leader's guide, and discussion questions. *Excellent for small-group or church class study.*

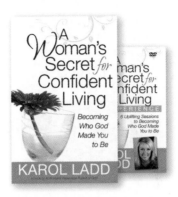

A Woman's Secret for Confident Living (book and DVD)
Becoming Who God Made You to Be

Bestselling author Karol Ladd shares powerful truths from the book of Colossians to help you make a vital shift in perspective. Knowing Christ and His greatness, and knowing who you are in Him, sets you on an exciting path to living—not in self-confidence, but *God*-confidence. You'll be helped to

- get rid of negative and self-defeating thoughts

- cultivate your potential, because you're valuable to Him

- shine with joy and assurance of what you bring to the world

Includes questions to bring depth and dimension to individual or group study.

In the complementary DVD version, Karol digs transforming truth out of the Scriptures in six positive, inspiring sessions such as "Transform Your Thinking," "Grow in Christ," and "Strengthen Your Relationships." *Helpful leader's guide included for group use.*

Unfailing Love
A Woman's Walk Through First John

It's easy to talk about filling your heart with God's love, but it's another thing to embrace His love, feel it, and allow it to color the fabric of your life. In this insightful journey through 1 John, Karol Ladd invites you to experience the reality of God's generous love. As you begin to grasp its height and depth...

- you're transformed, seeing yourself and your circumstances in a fresh new light.

- you get a truer picture of Jesus, God's Son, in a way that helps you navigate the false loves, temporary pleasures, and seductions of today's culture.

- you're able to graciously, compassionately, and creatively love others by your words and actions.

God is Light, Life, and Love. As you embrace Him, you'll experience how He gives meaning to your existence, victory over your discouragements, and hope to the world.

To learn more about Harvest House books and
to read sample chapters, visit our website:

www.harvesthousepublishers.com

HARVEST HOUSE PUBLISHERS
EUGENE, OREGON